TRACE LETTERS OF THE ALPHABET

WITH SIGHT WORDS

By: Activity Nest

activitynest.org

This book is dedicated to the children of the world. May your hearts be full of joy.

If you enjoy the book, please consider leaving a review wherever you bought it.

ISBN: 978-1-951791-32-2

Get All Our New Releases For FREE!

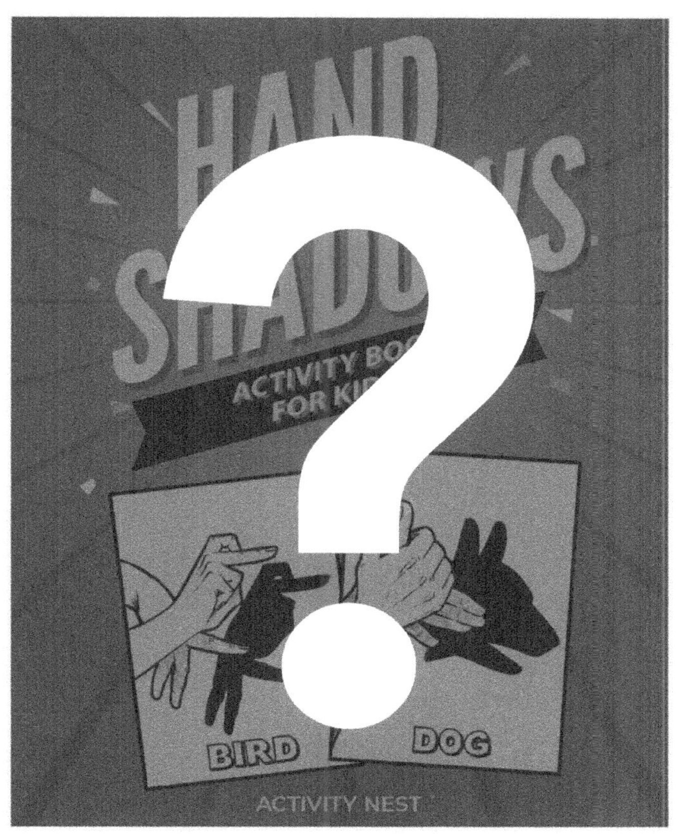

Sign up to our VIP Newsletter to get all of our

future releases absolutely free!

www.activitynest.org/free

Alphabet

Trace the letters

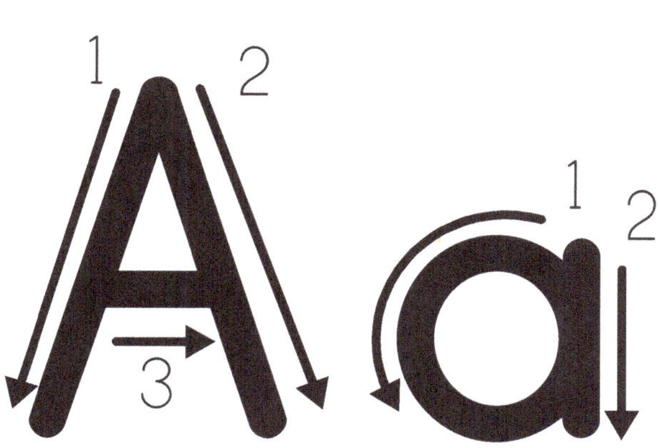

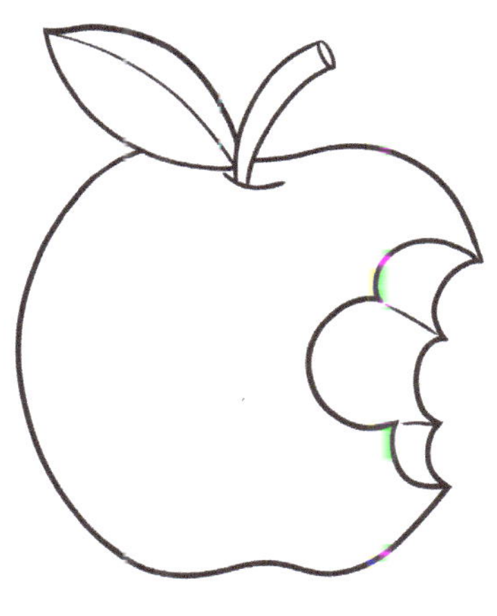

Apple

Apple

a a a a a a a a a a

A A A A A A A A

a a a a a a a a

a a a

A A A

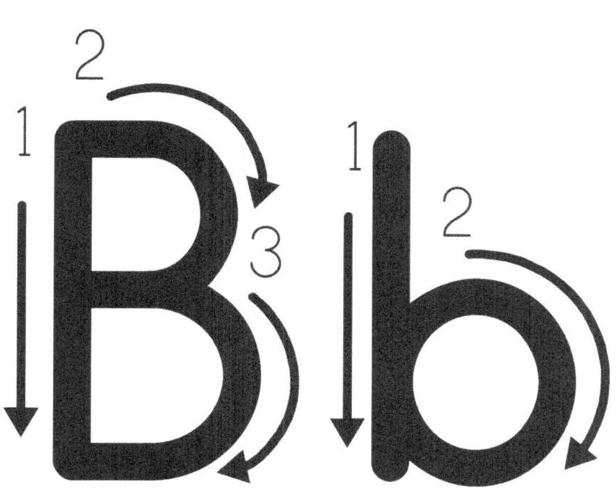

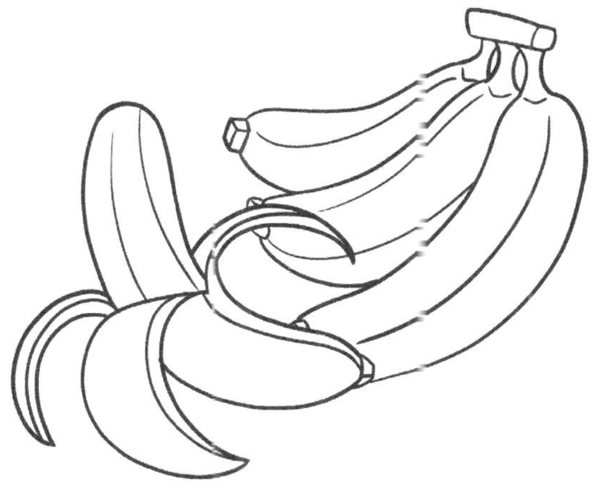

Banana

Banana

b b

B B

b b

b b

b b

b b

B B

B B

B B

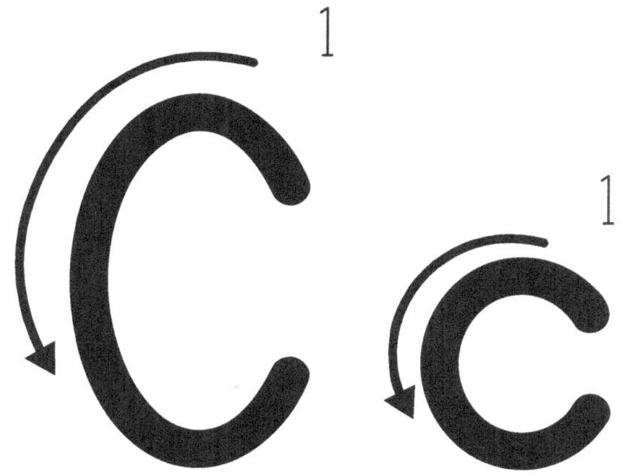

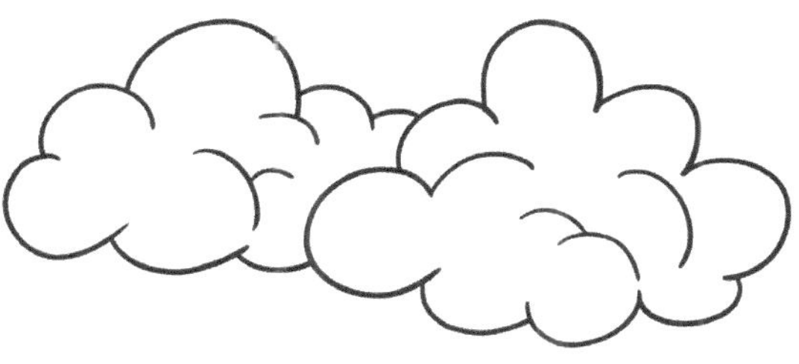

Cloud

Cloud

c c c c c c c c

C C C C C C C

c c c c c c c c

c c

c c

c c

C C

C C

C C

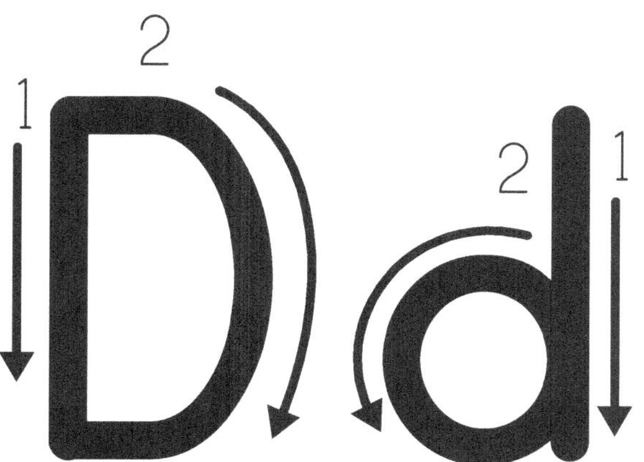

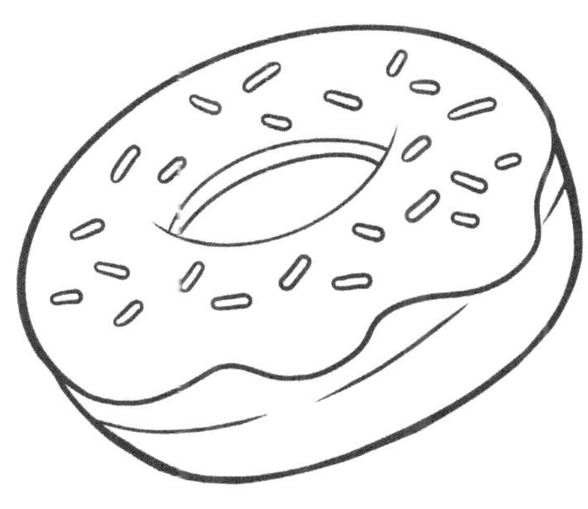

Donut

Donut

d d d d d d d

D D D D D D D

d d d d d d d

d d

d d

d d

D D

D D

D D

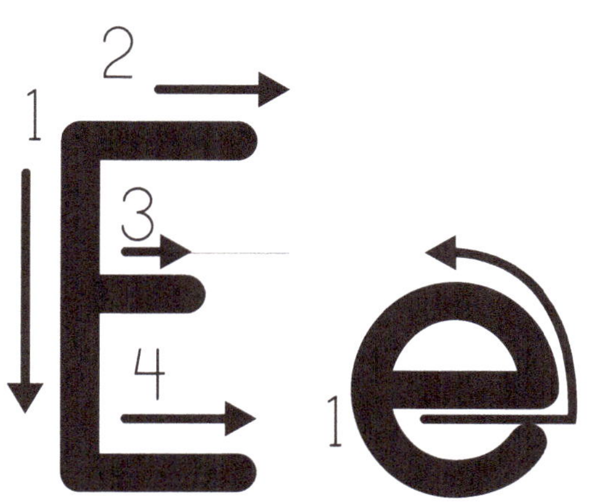

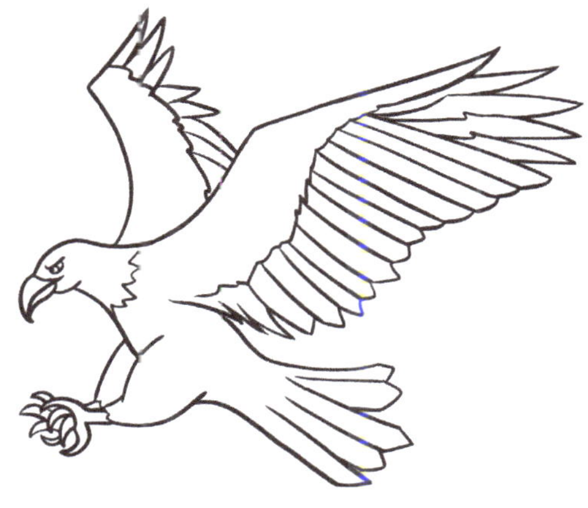

Eagle

Eagle

e e e e e e e e

E E

e e e e e e e e

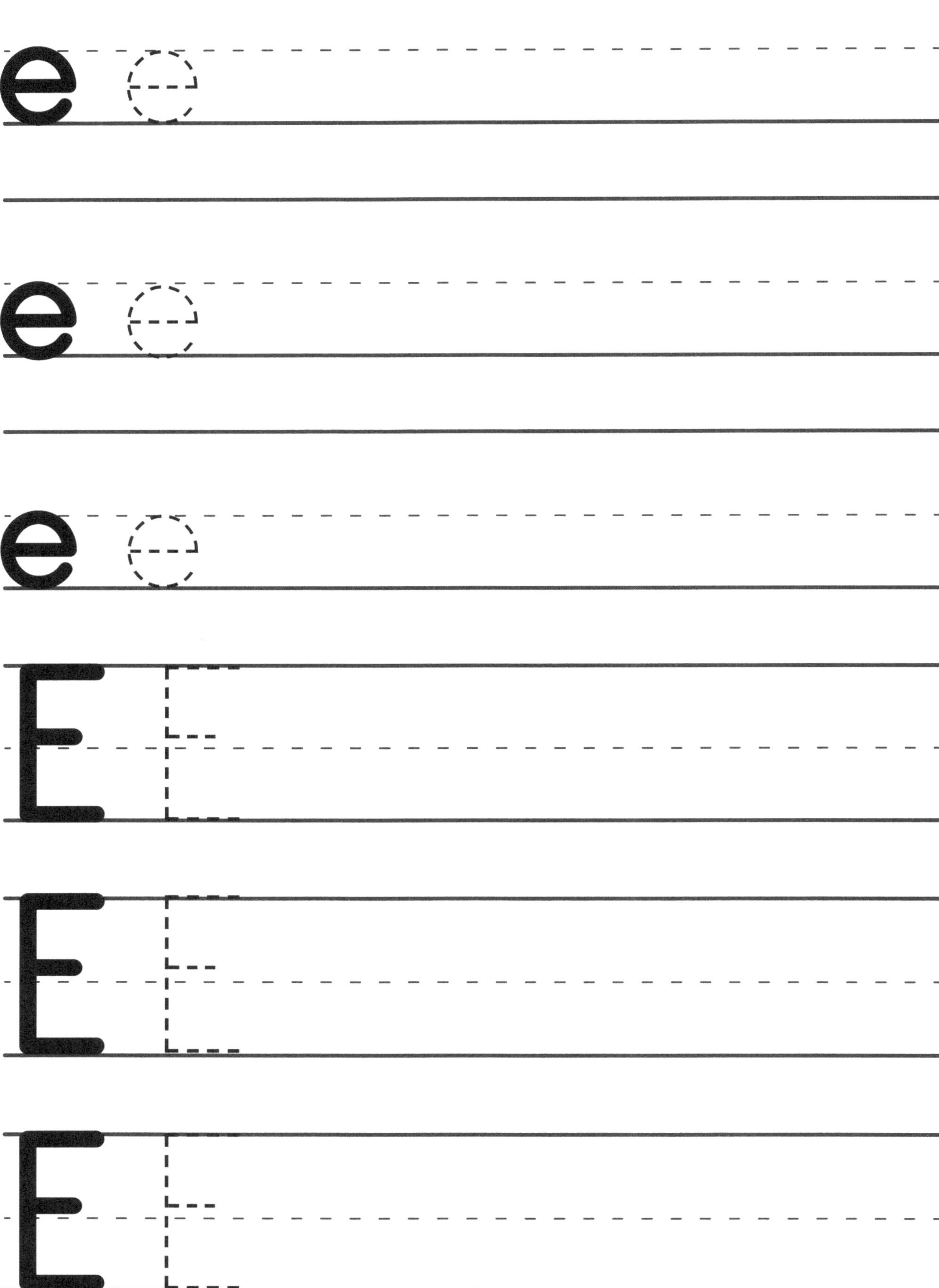

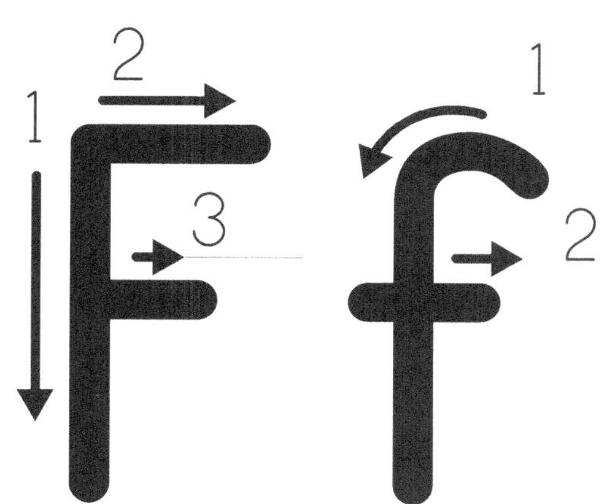
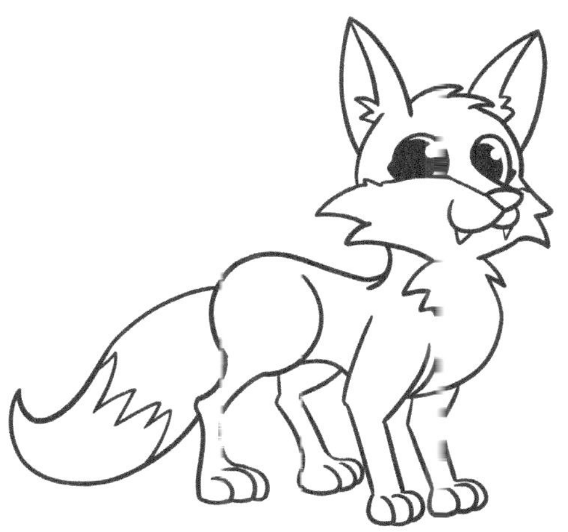

Fox

Fox

f f

F F

f f

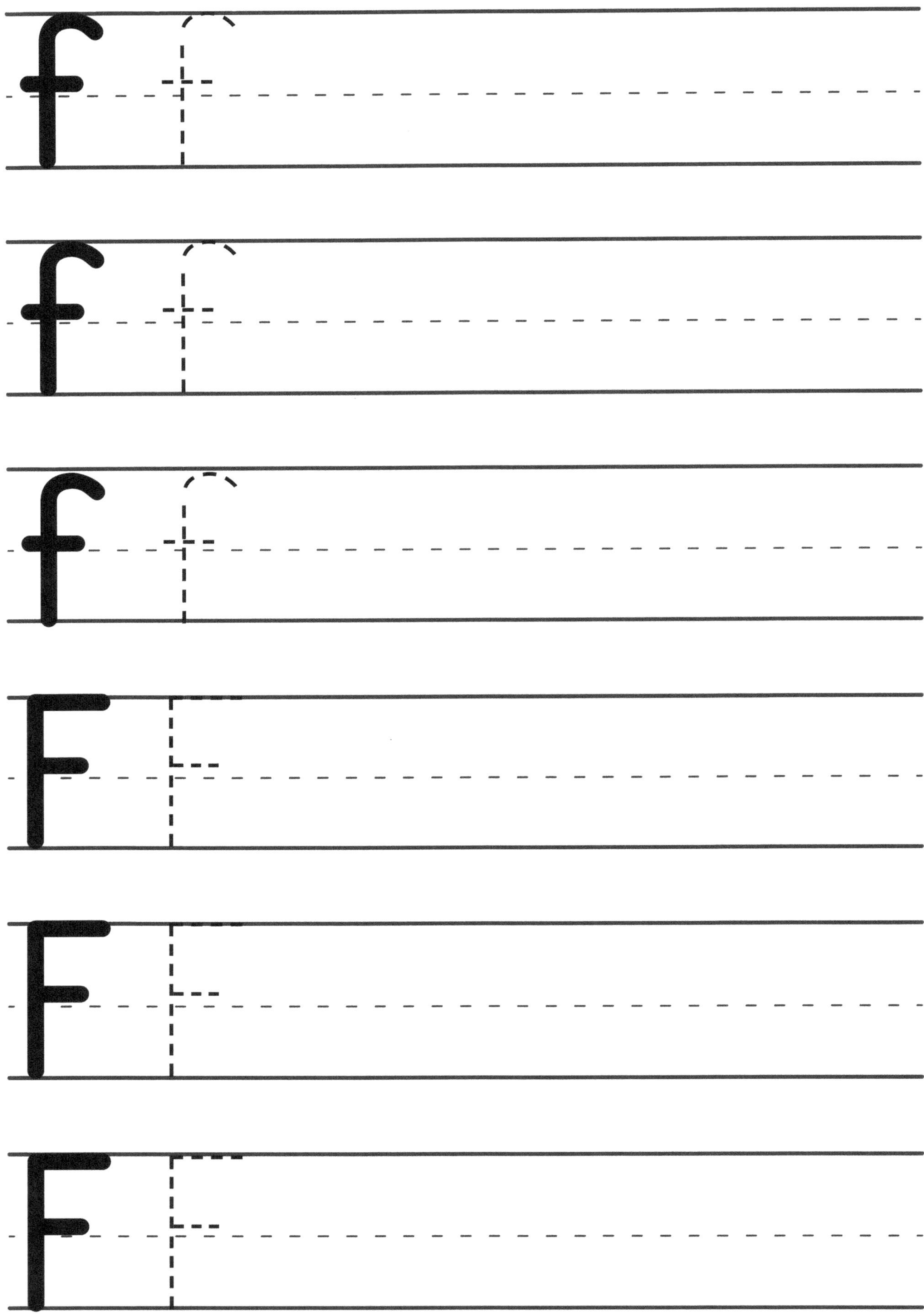

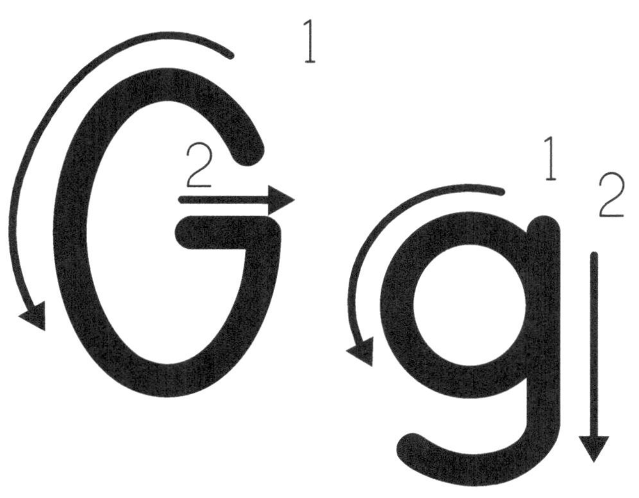

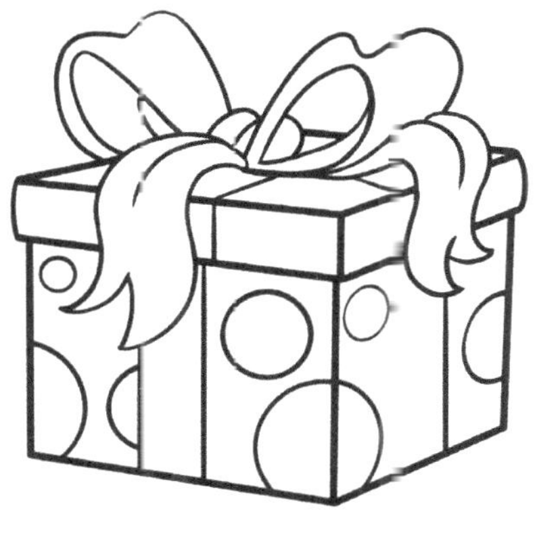

Gift

Gift

g g

G G

g g

g

g

g

G

G

G

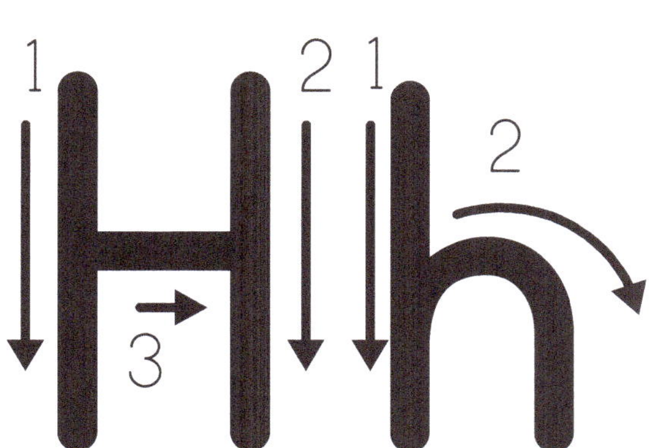

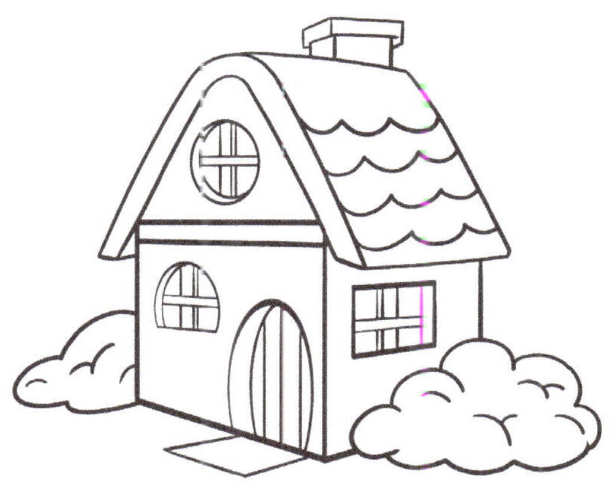

House

House

h h

H H

h h

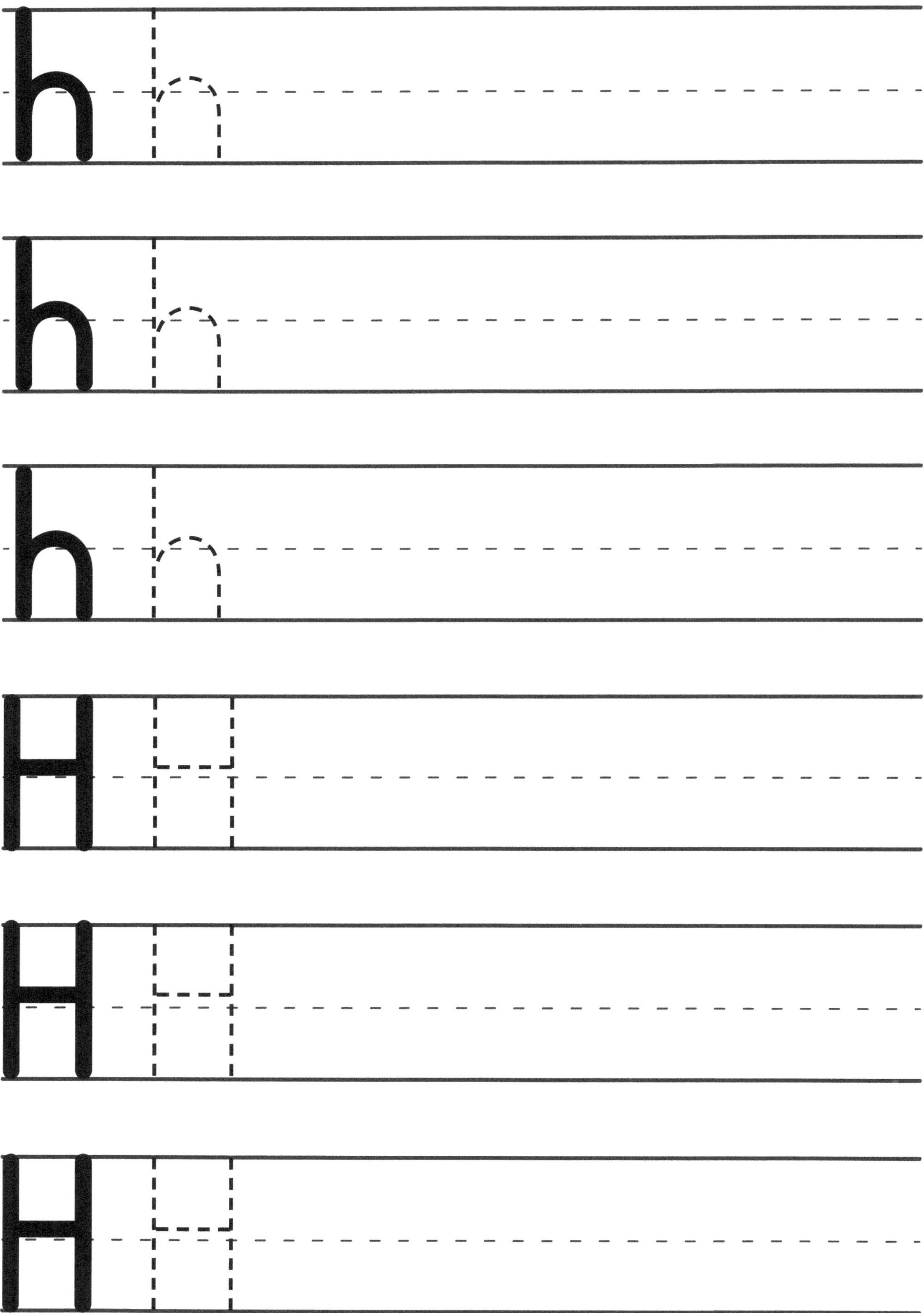

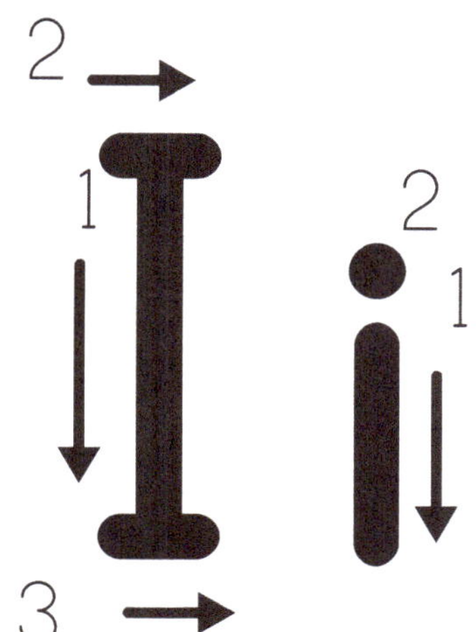

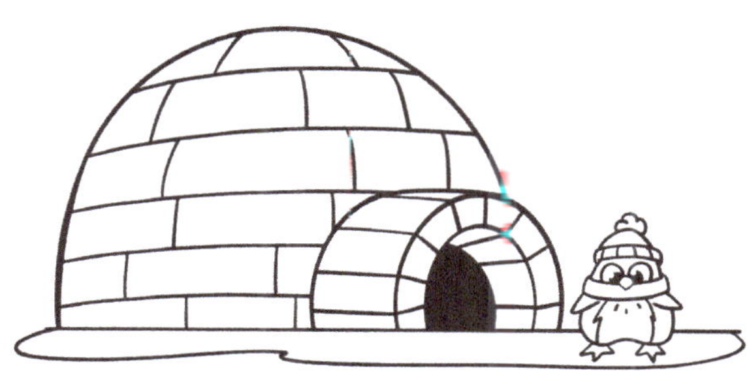

Igloo

Igloo

i i

I I

i i

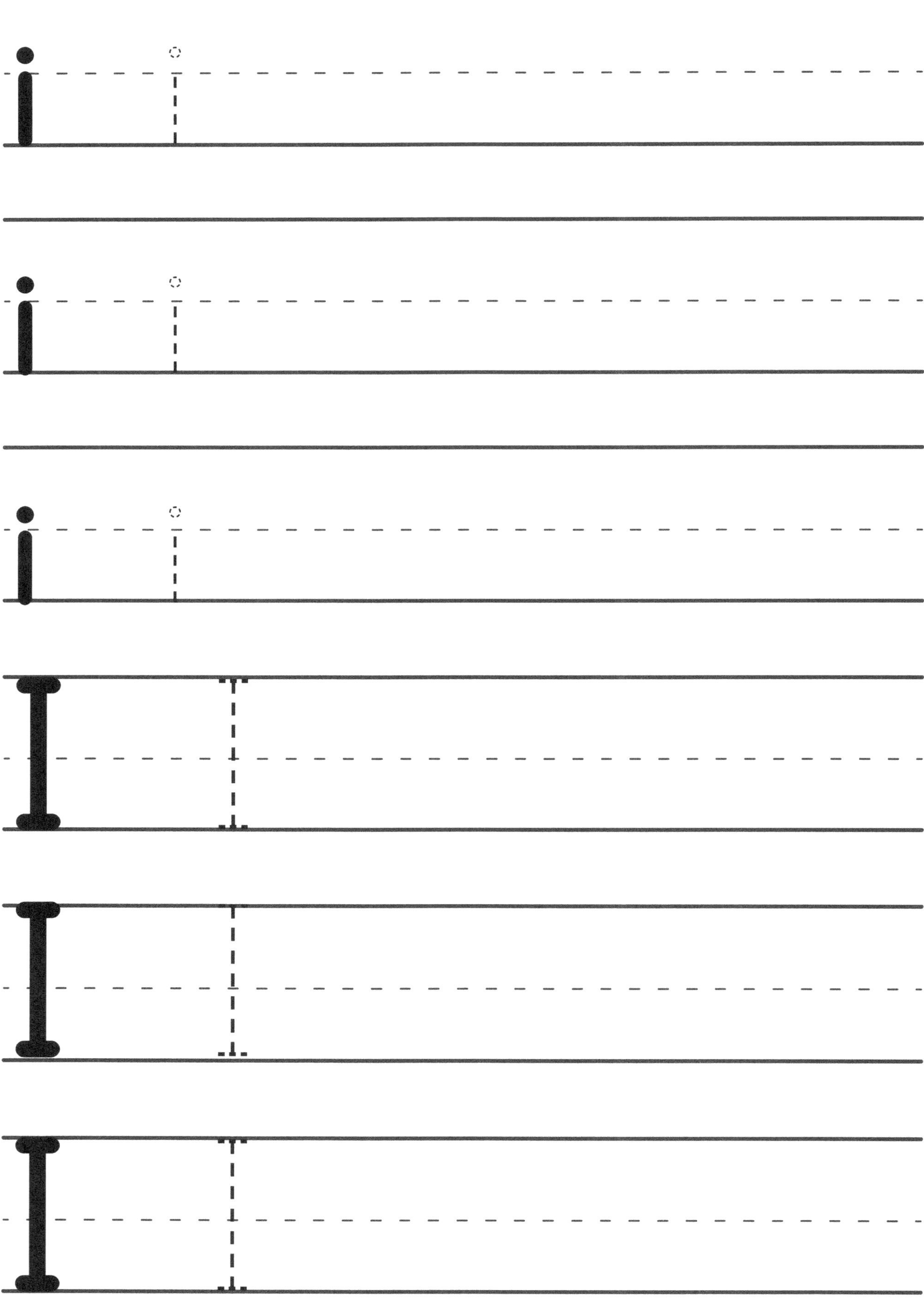

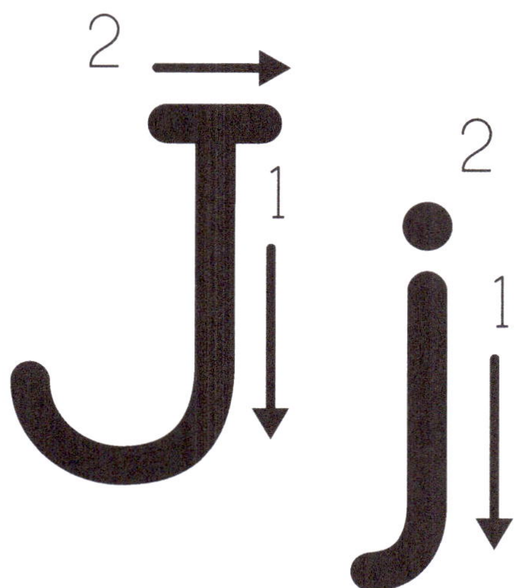

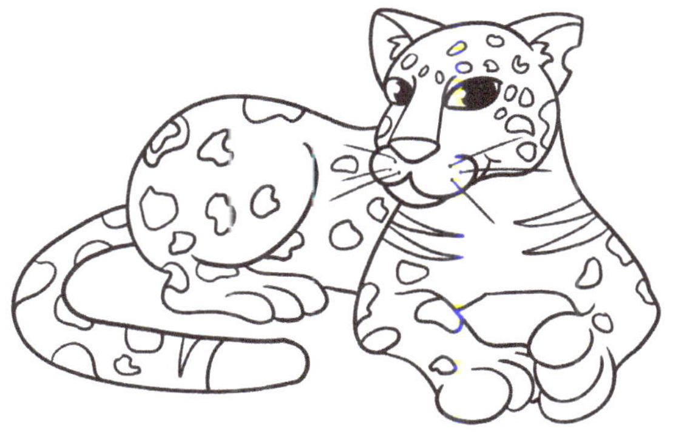

Jaguar

Jaguar

j j

J J

j j

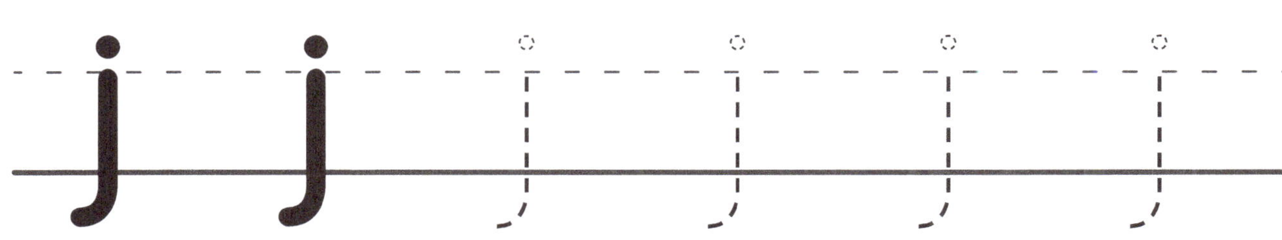

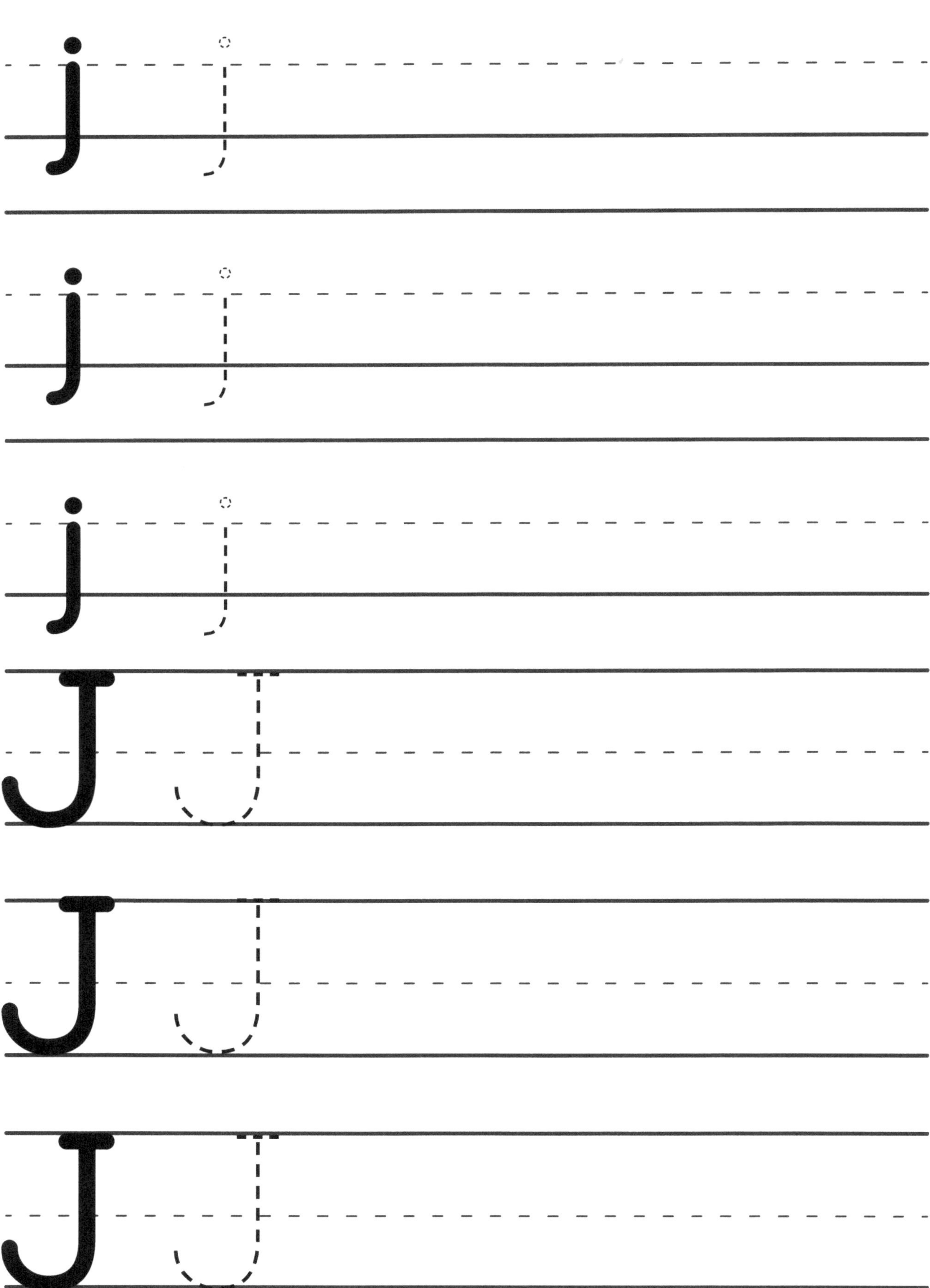

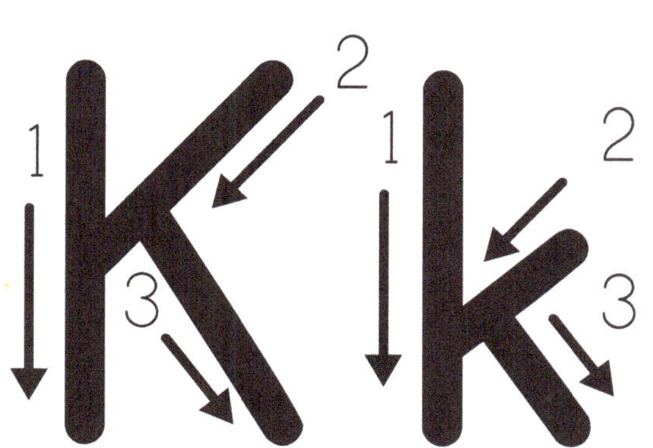

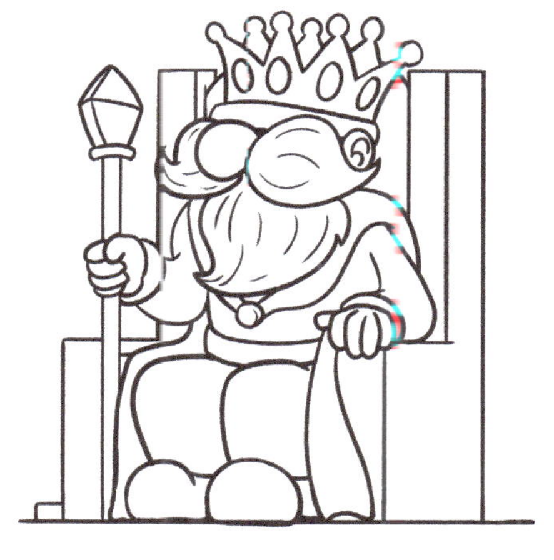

King

King

k k

K K

k k

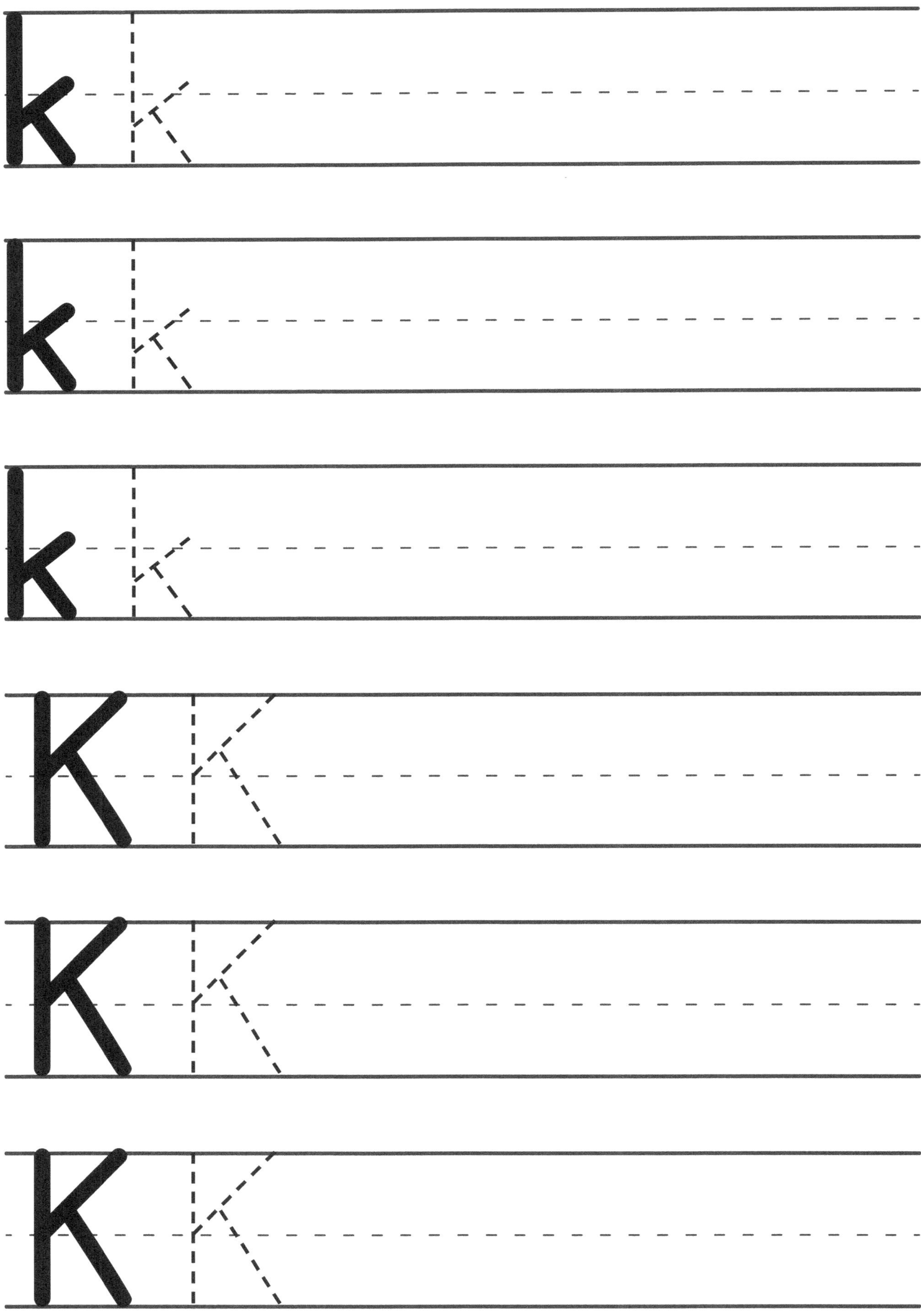

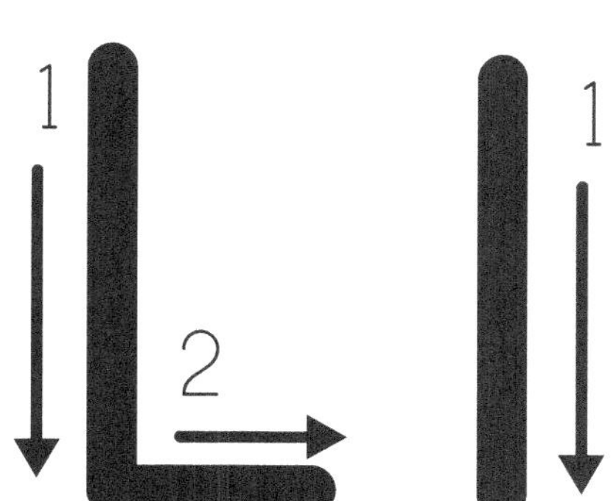

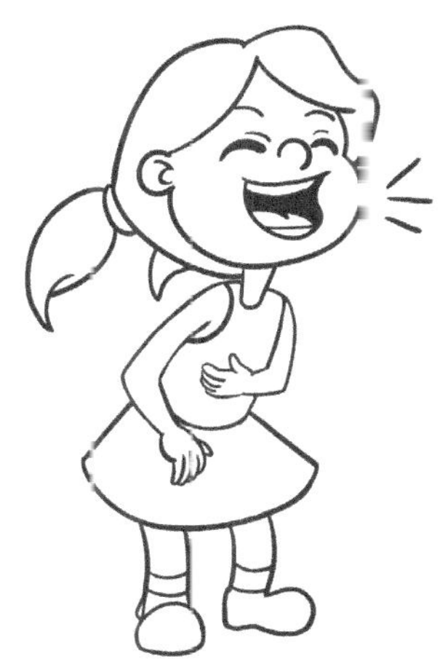

Laugh

Laugh

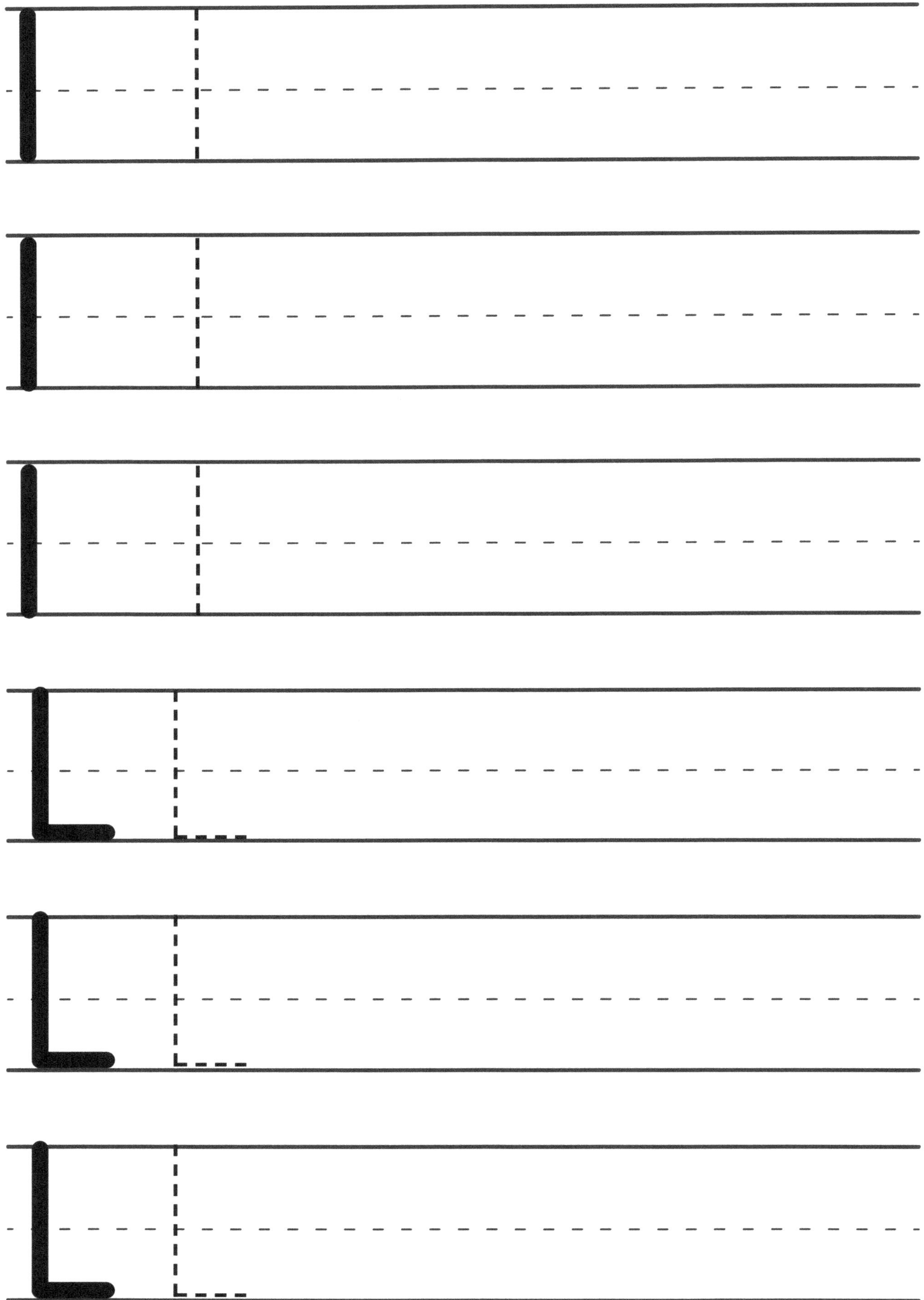

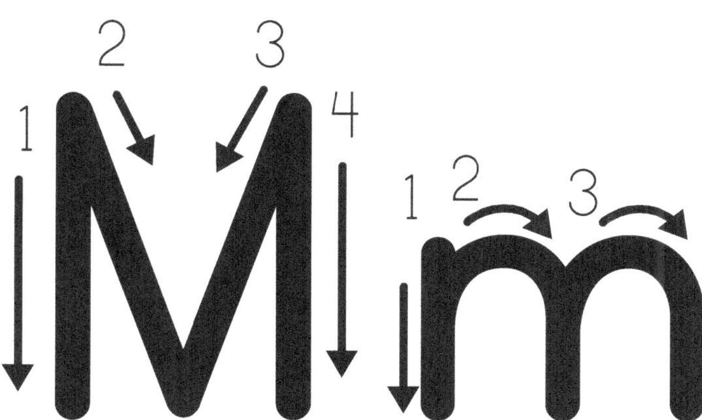 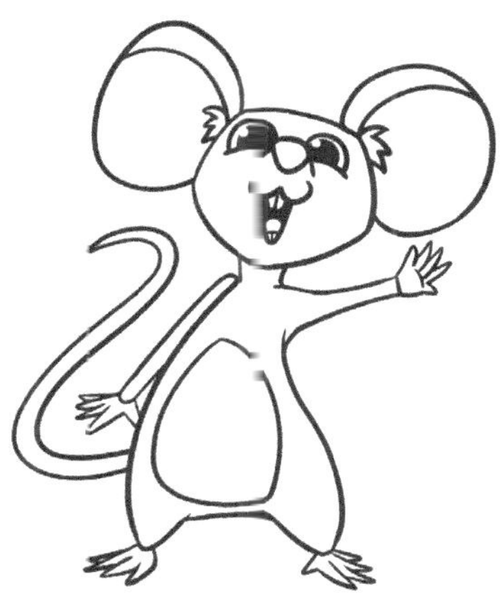

Mouse

Mouse

m m m m m m

M M M M M M

m m m m m m

m m

m m

m m

M M

M M

M M

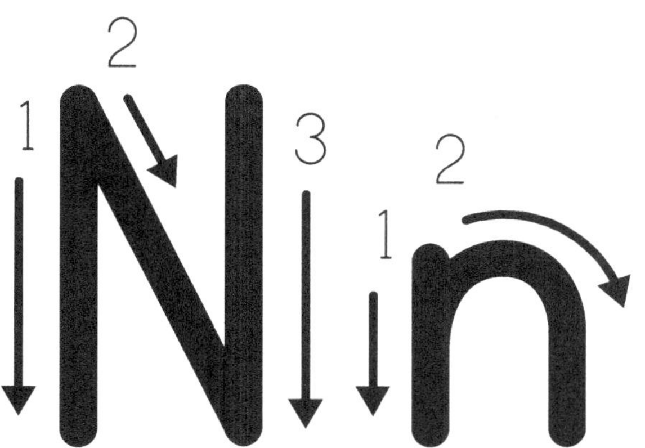

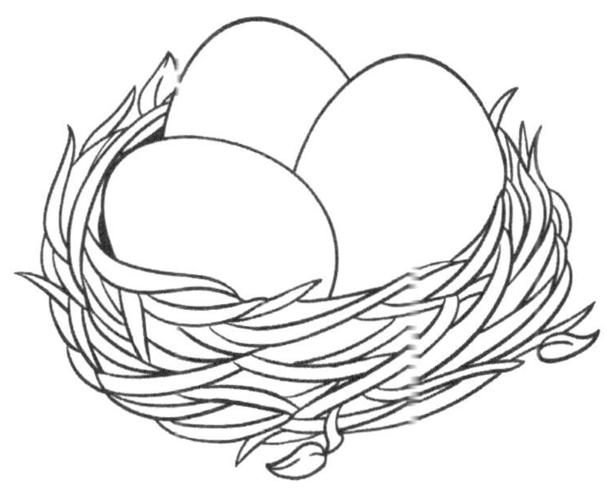

Nest

Nest

n n

N N

n n

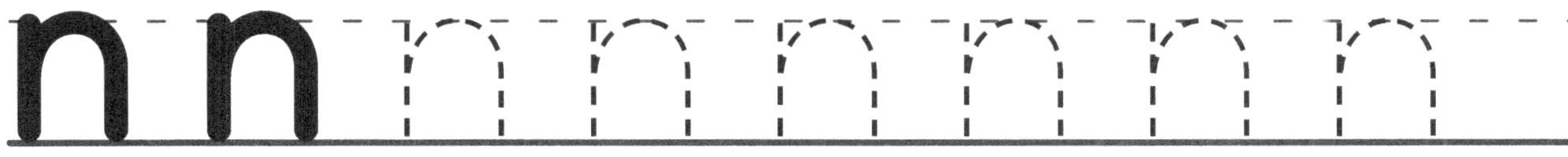

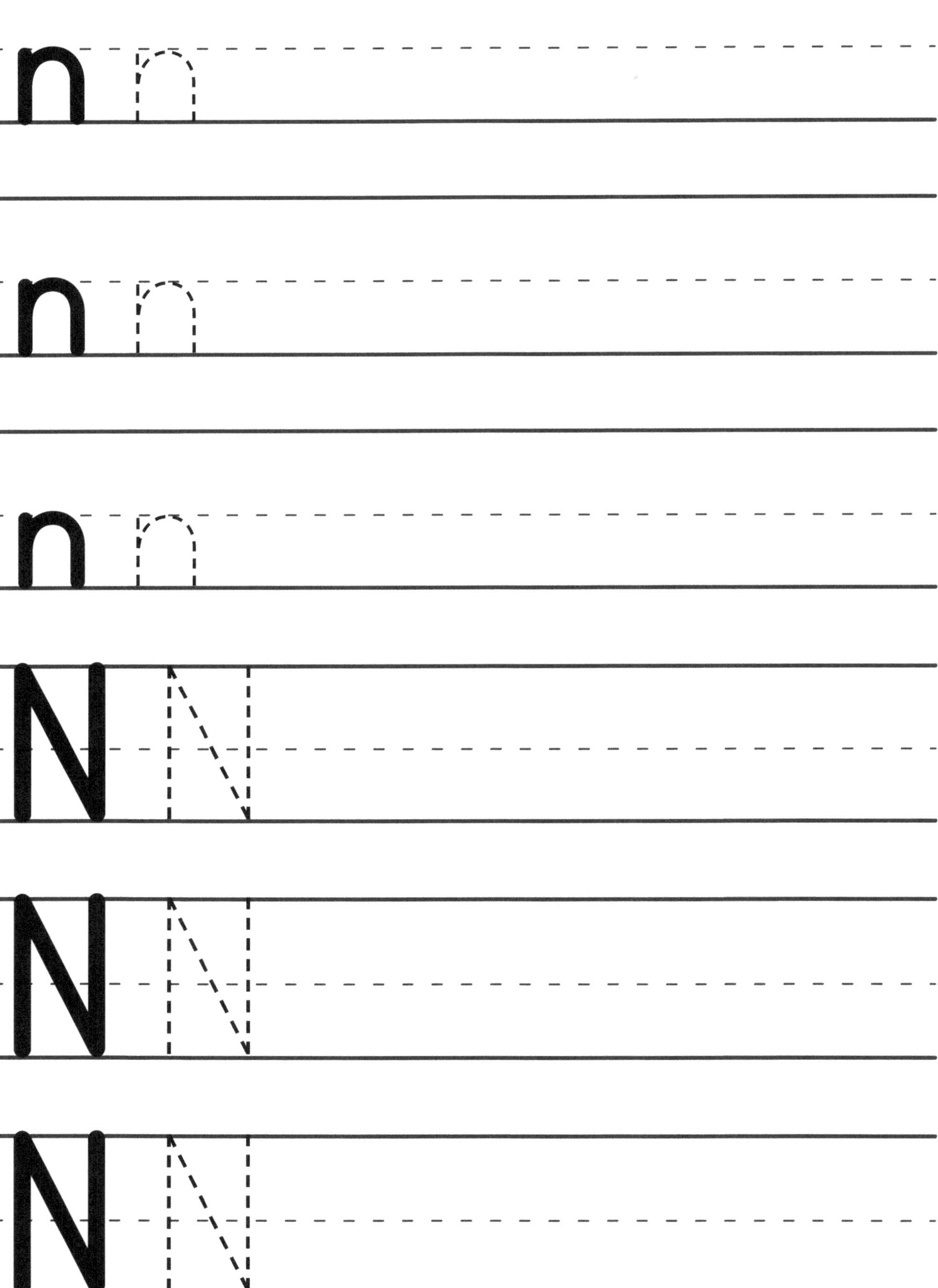

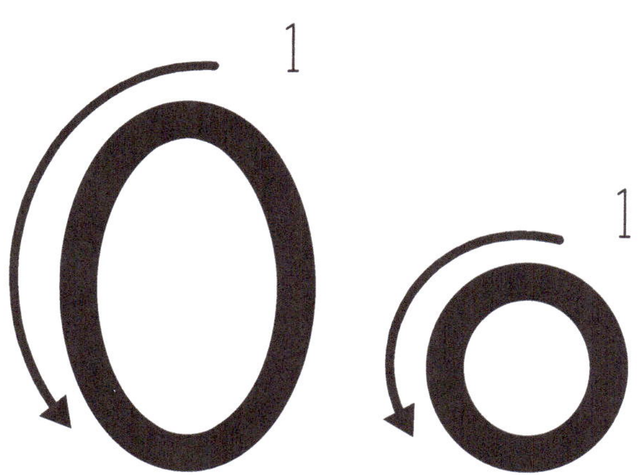

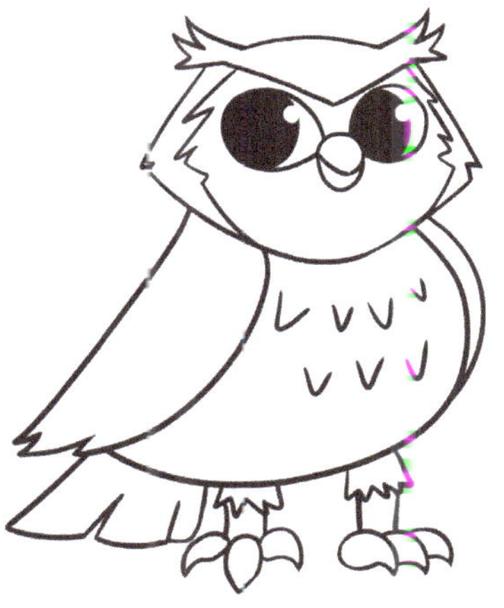

Owl

O w l

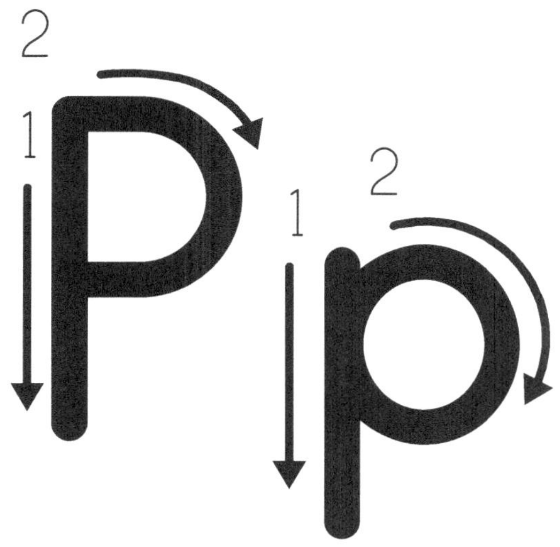

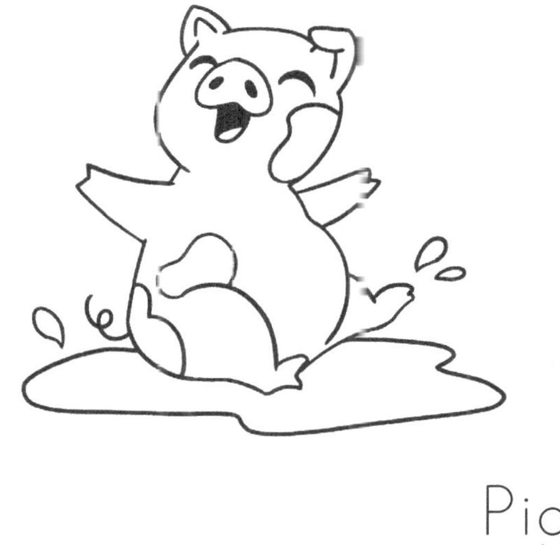

Pig

P i g

p p o o o o o o

P P P P P P P P

p p o o o o o o

p p
p p
p p
P P
P P
P P

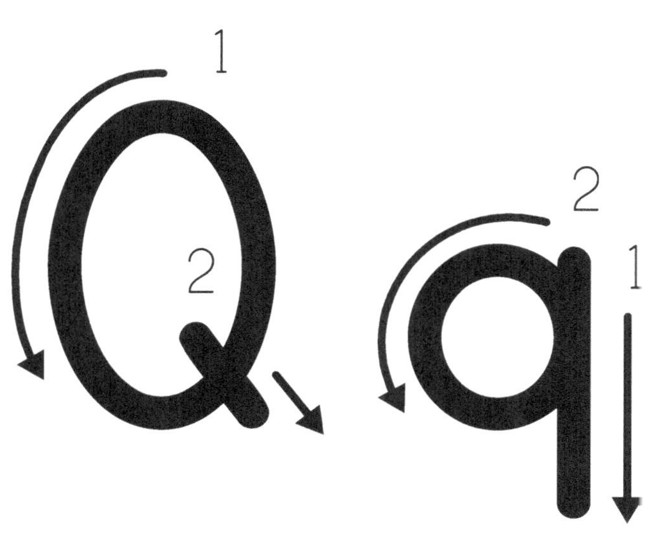

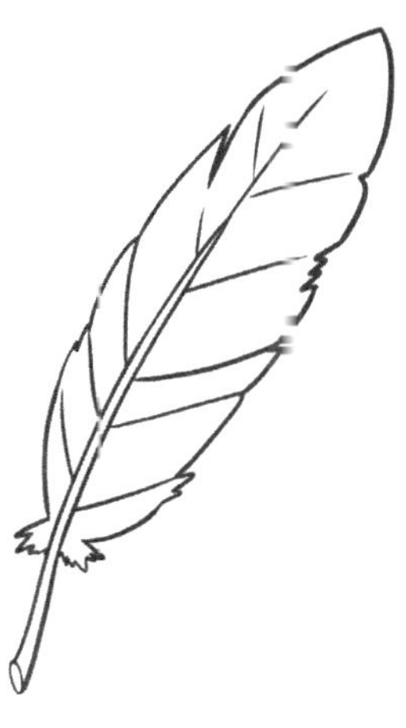

Quill

Quill

q q ɑ ɑ ɑ ɑ ɑ ɑ

Q Q Q Q Q Q Q Q

q q ɑ ɑ ɑ ɑ ɑ ɑ

q

q

q

Q

Q

Q

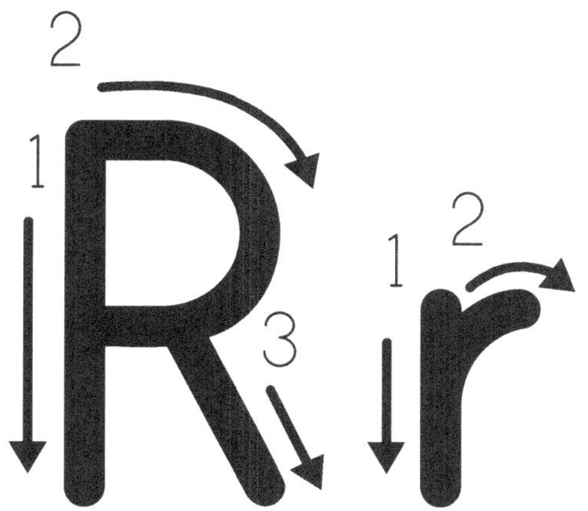

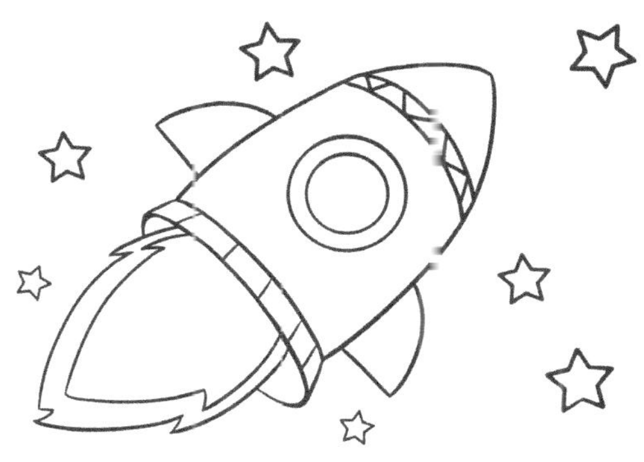

Rocket

Rocket

r r

R R

r r

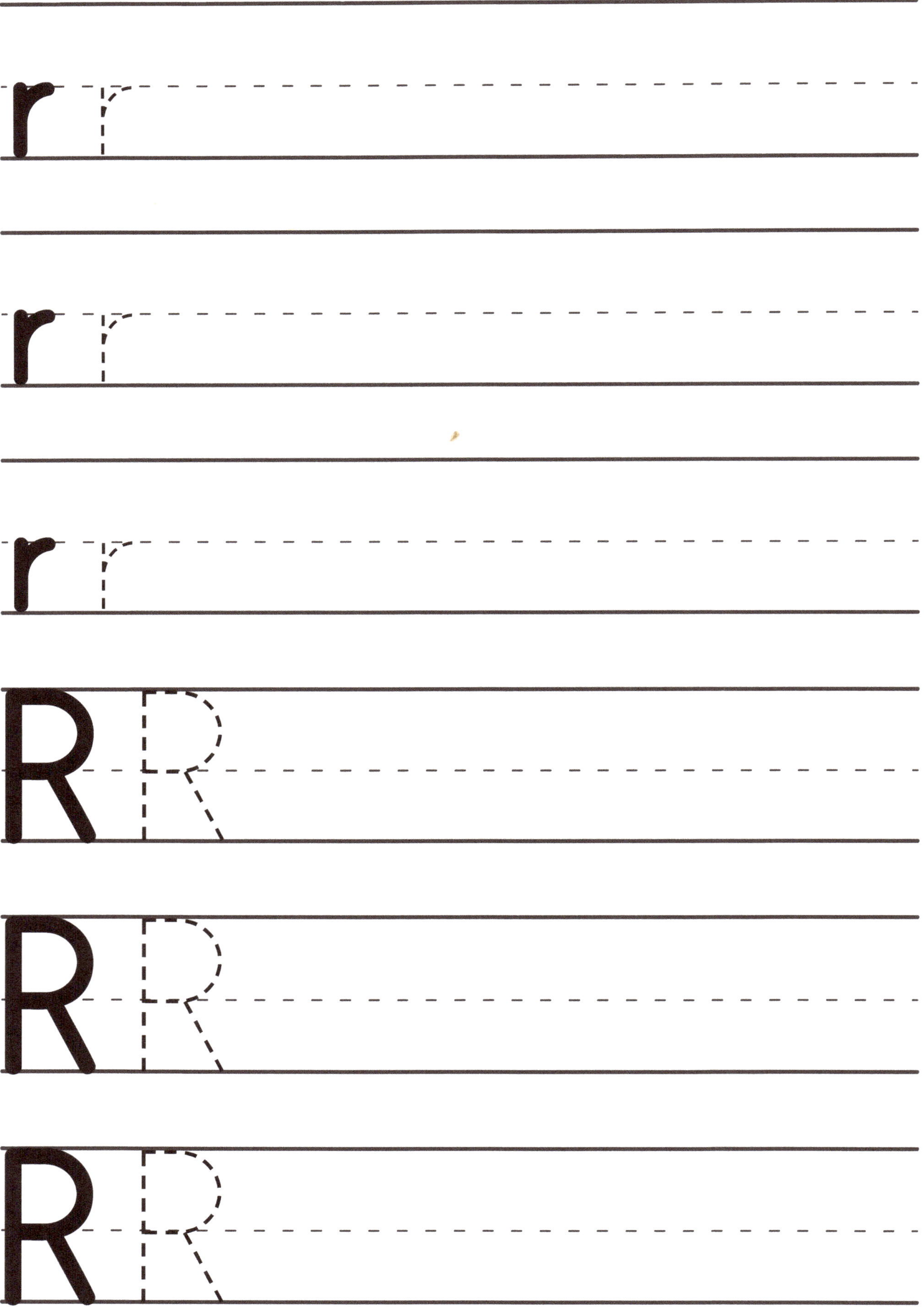

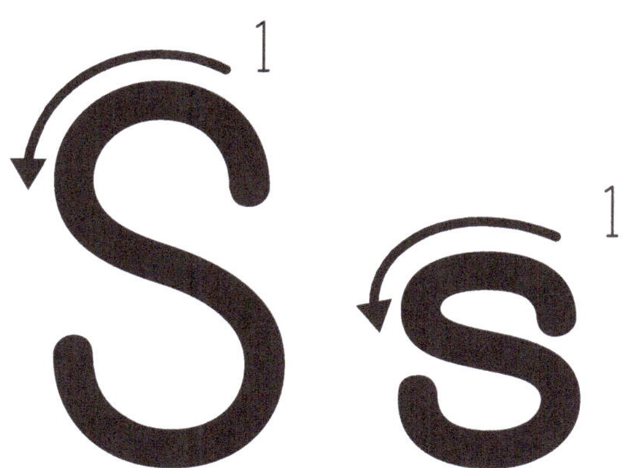

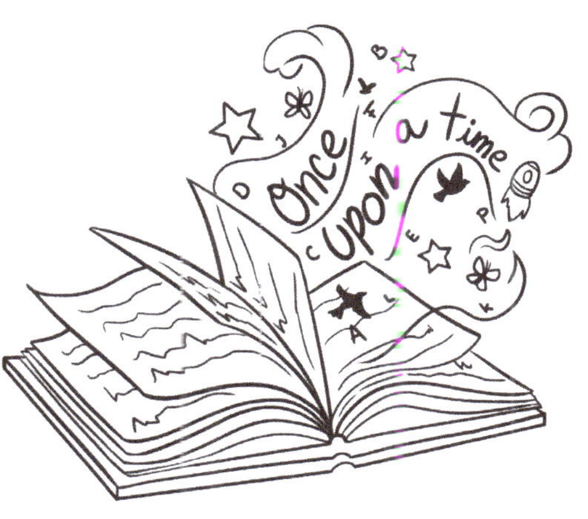

Story

Story

s s s s s s s s

S S S S S S

s s s s s s s

s s

s s

s s

S S

S S

S S

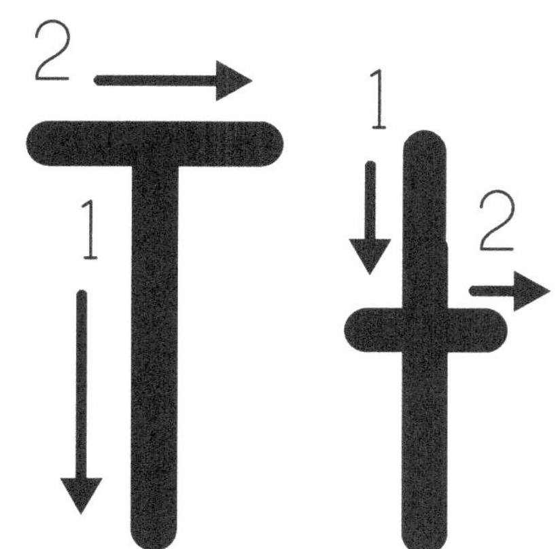

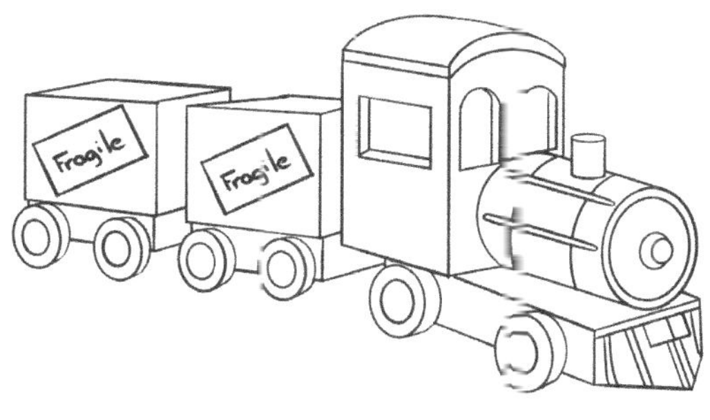

Train

Train

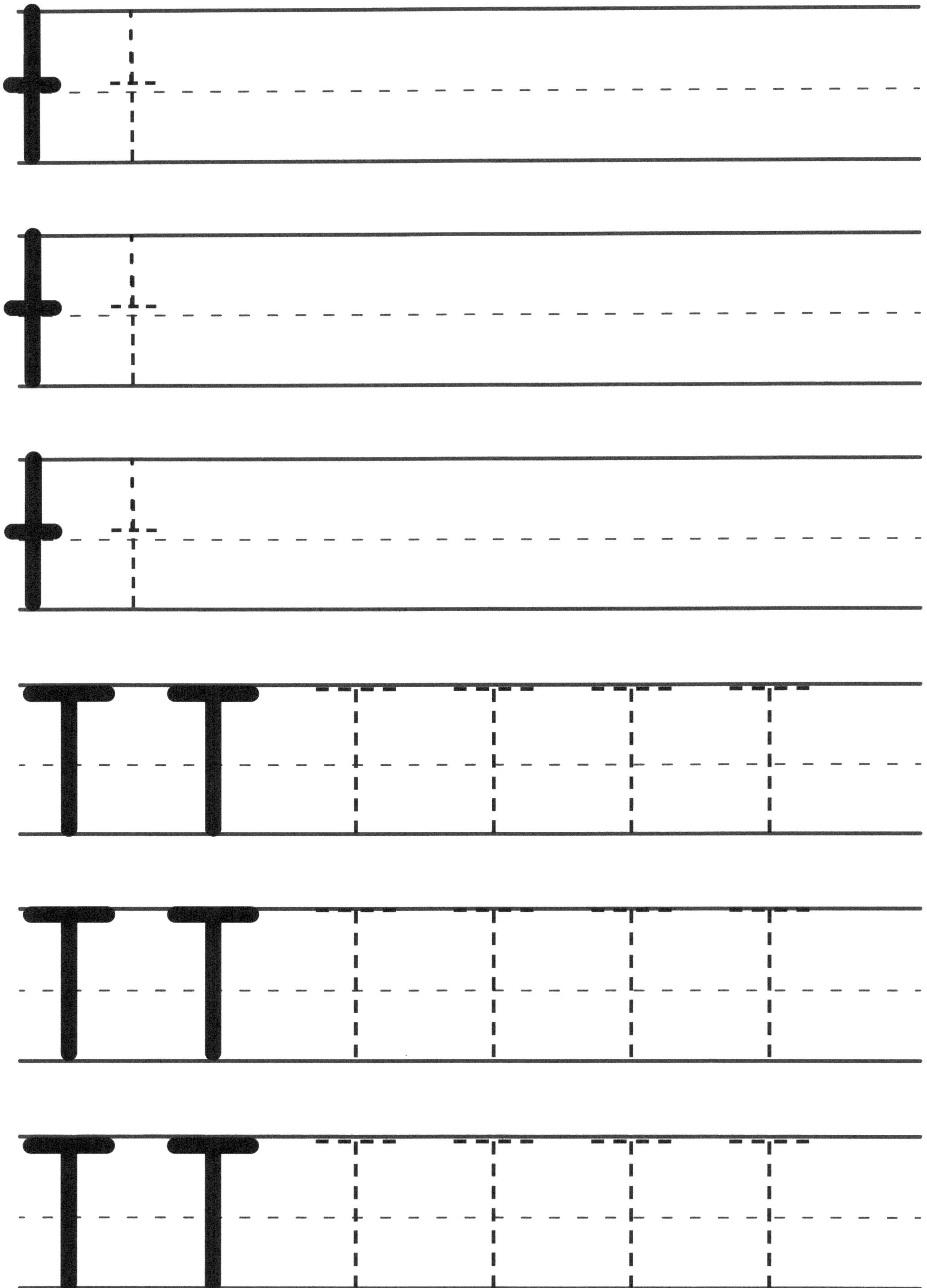

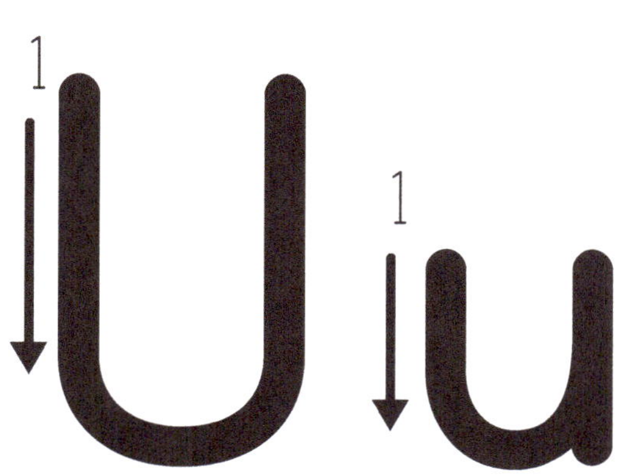

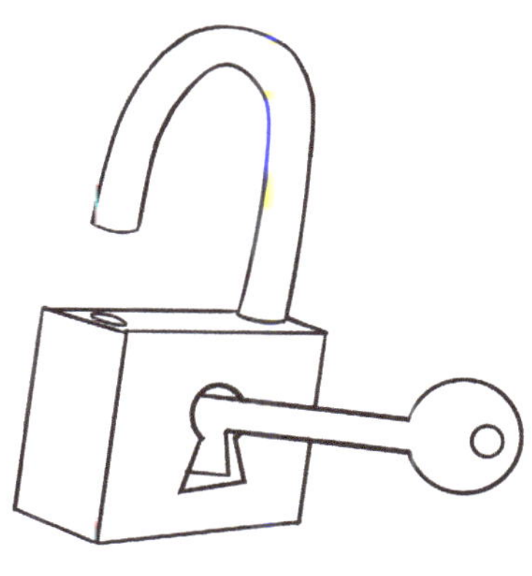

Unlock

Unlock

u u

U U

u u

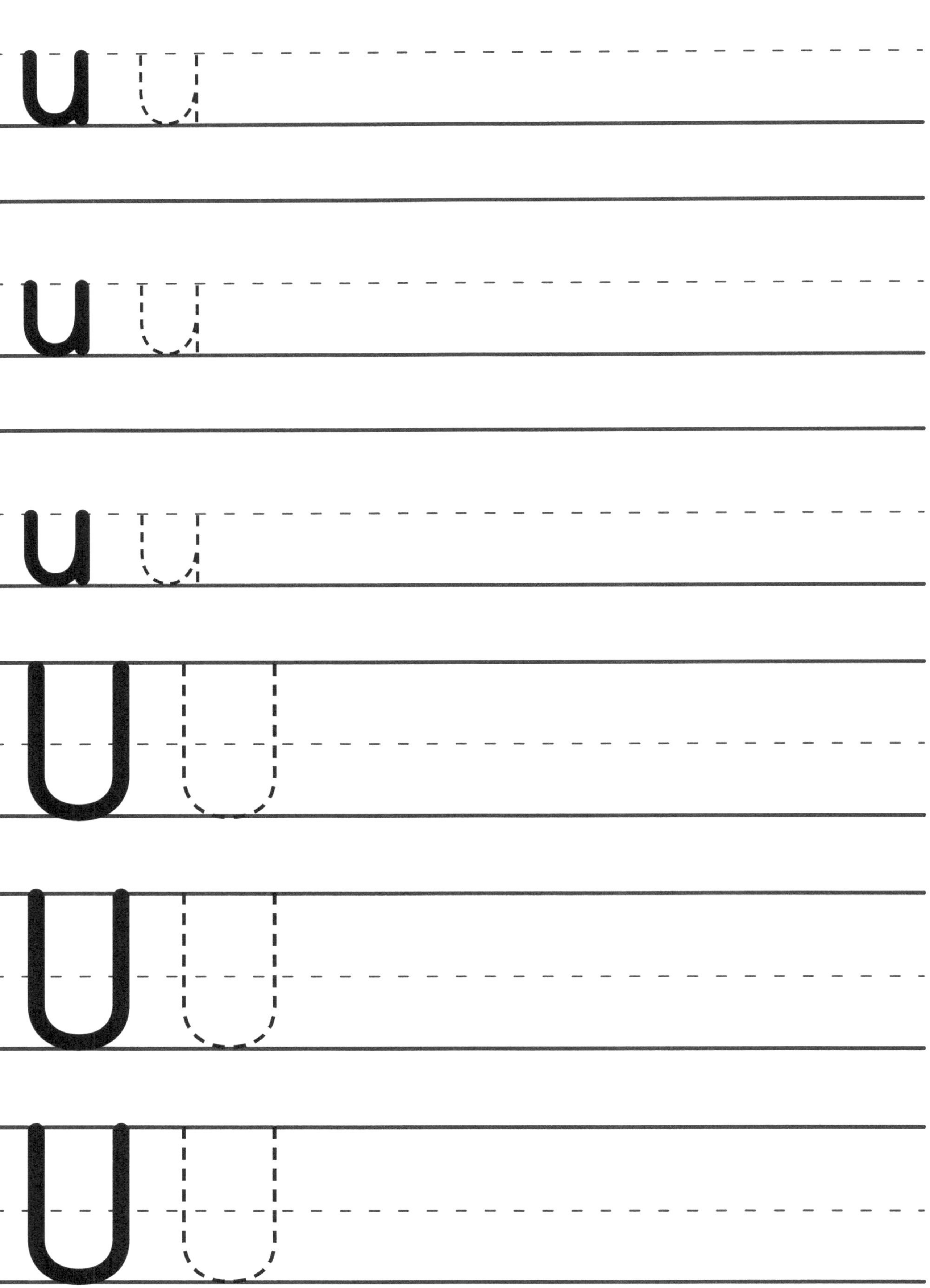

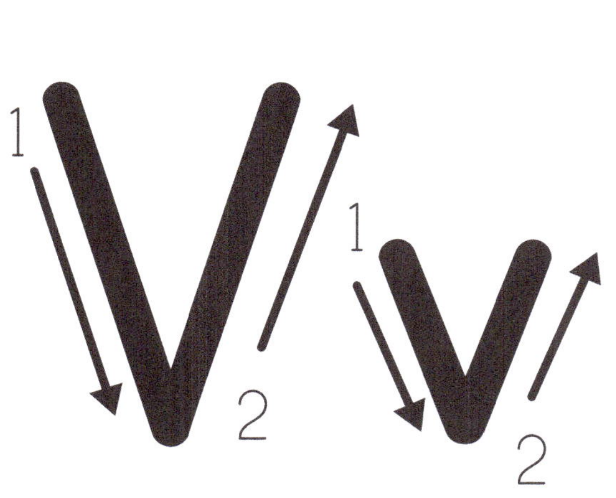

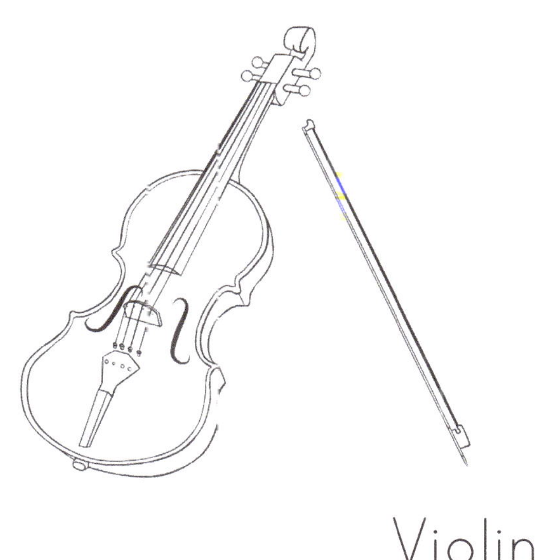

Violin

Violin

V V v v v v v v v

VV V V V V V V

v v v v v v v v v

V v

V v

V v

V V

V V

V V

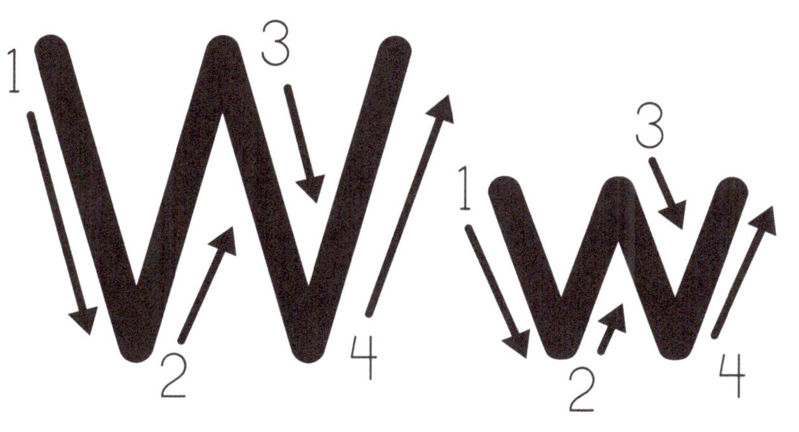

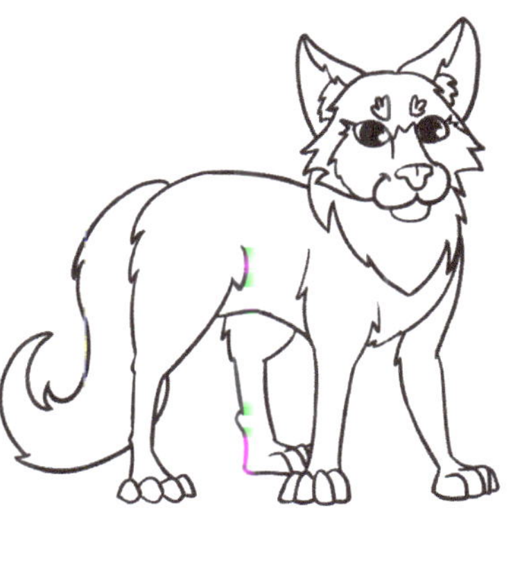

Wolf

Wolf

w w w w w w w

W W W W W

w w w w w w

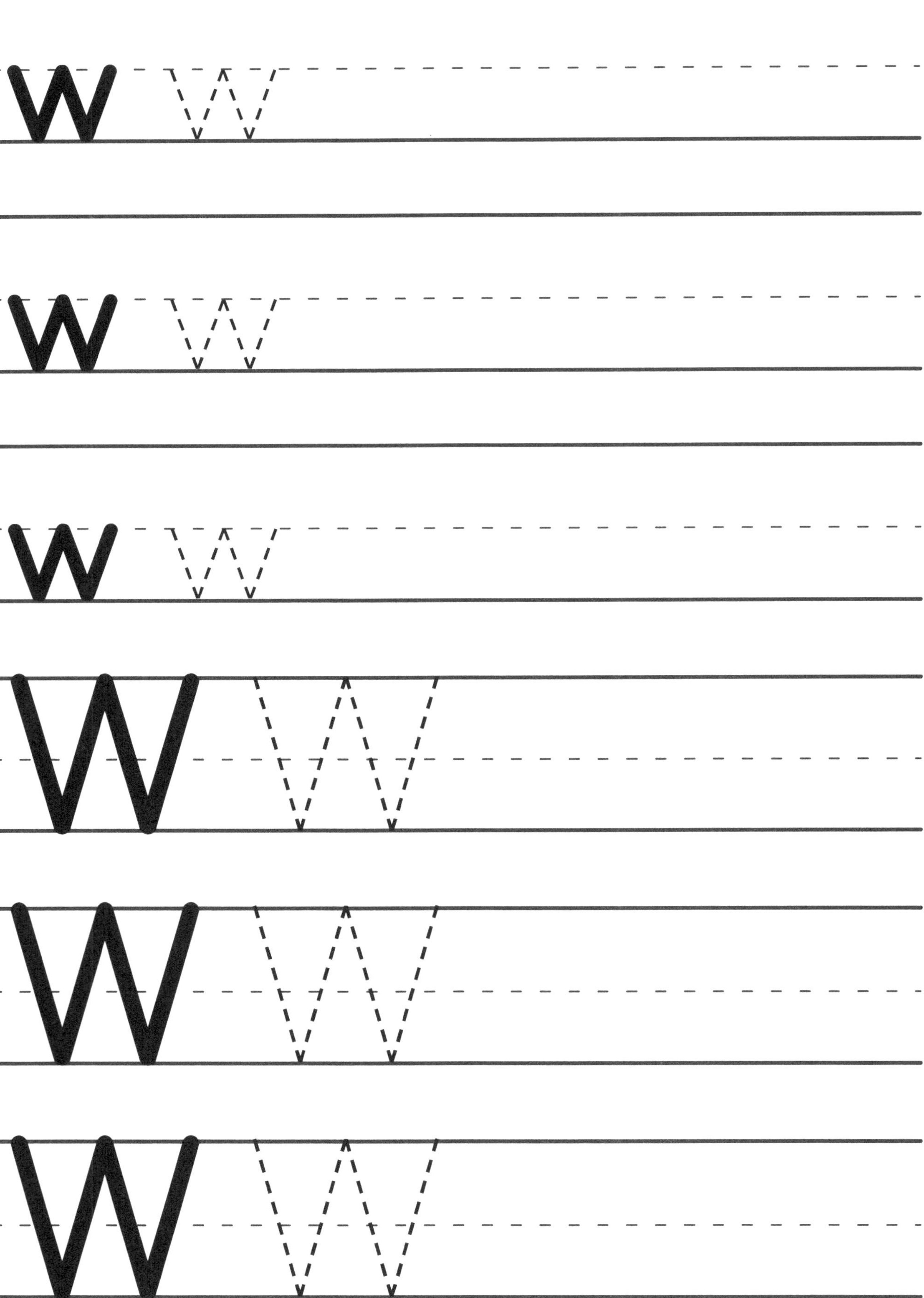

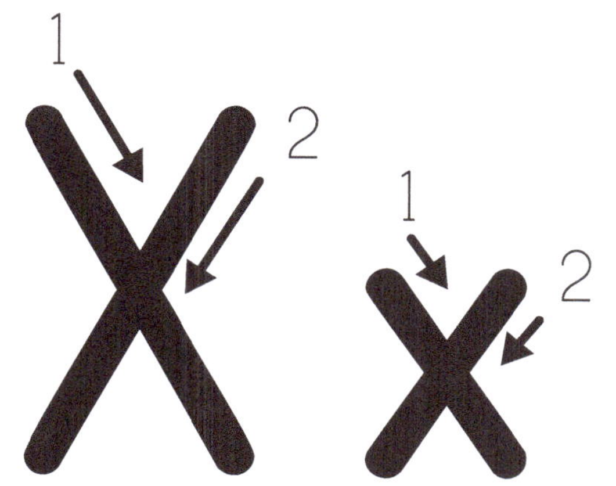

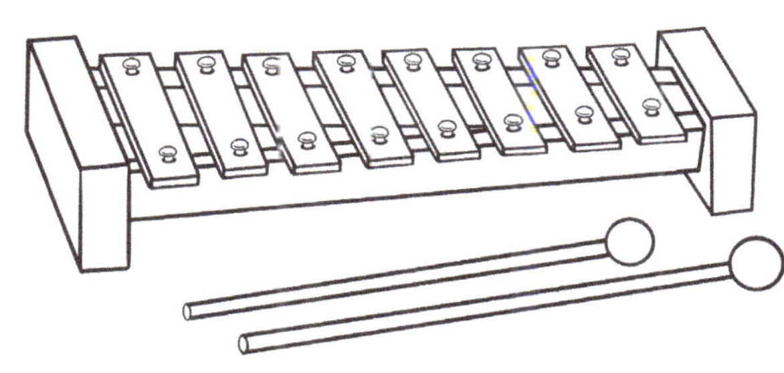

Xylophone

Xylophone

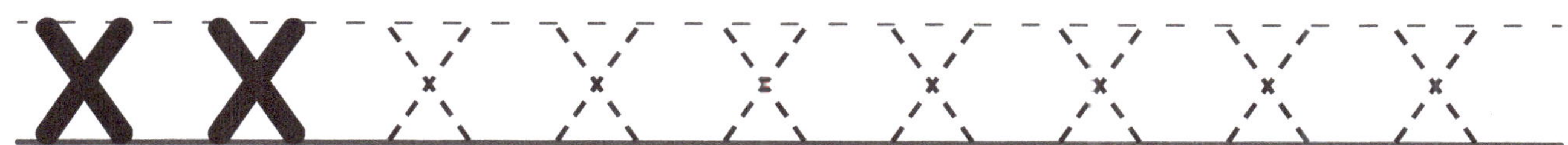

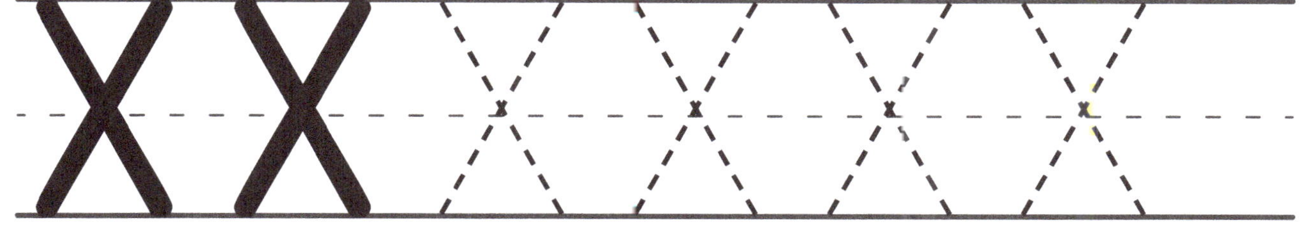

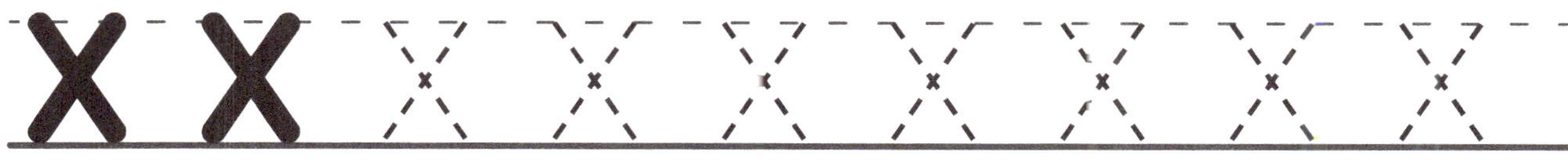

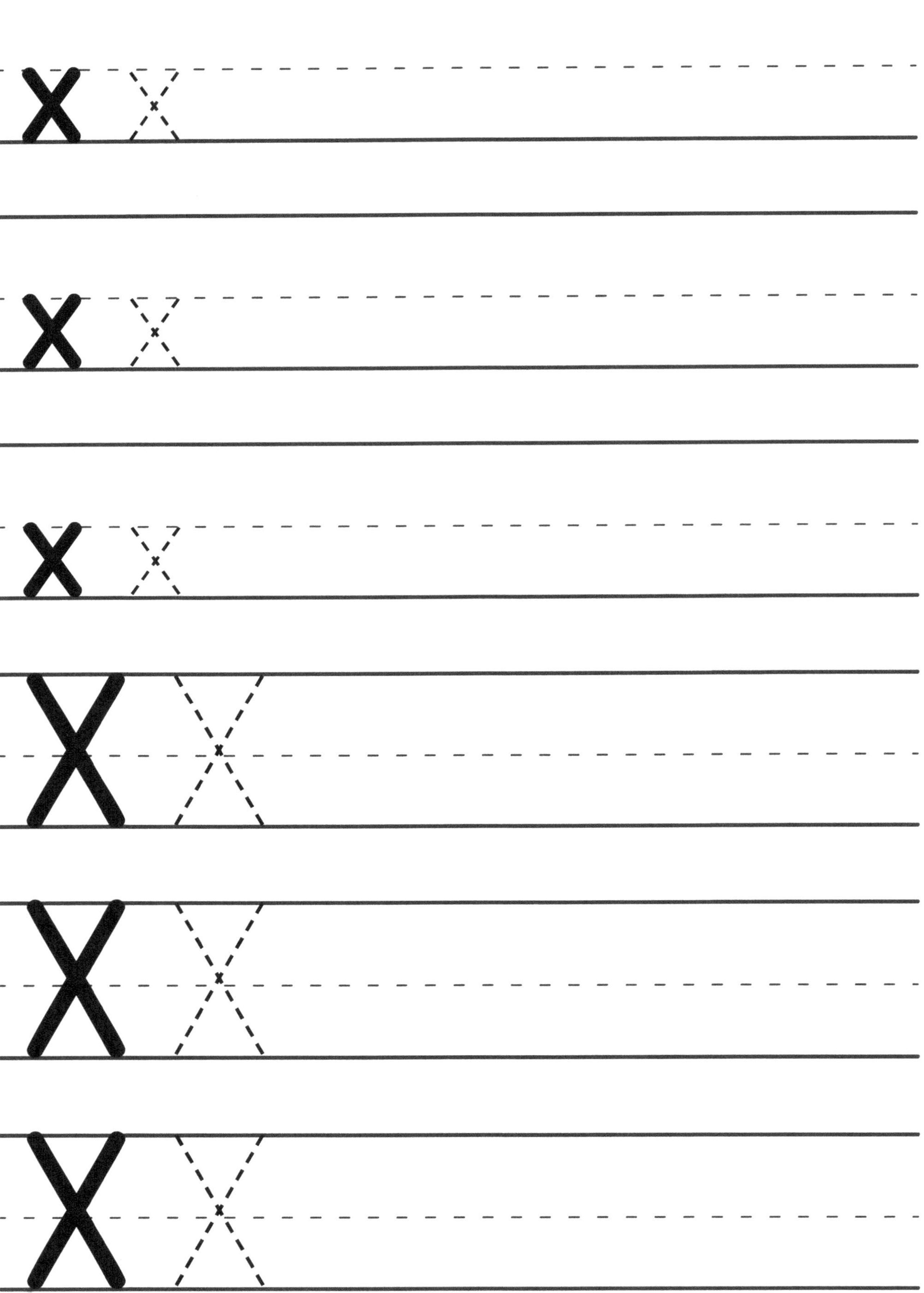

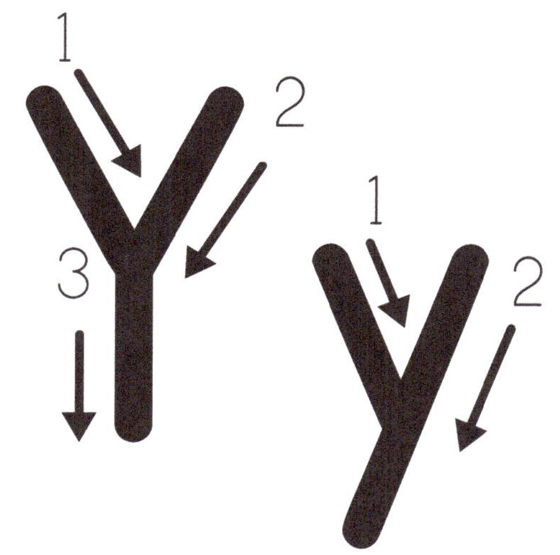

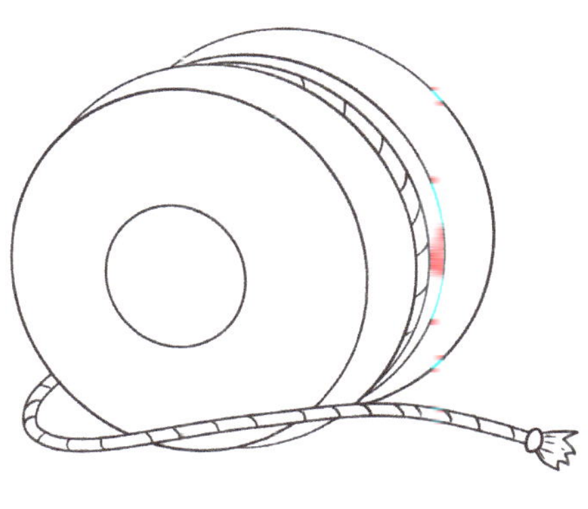

Yoyo

Yoyo

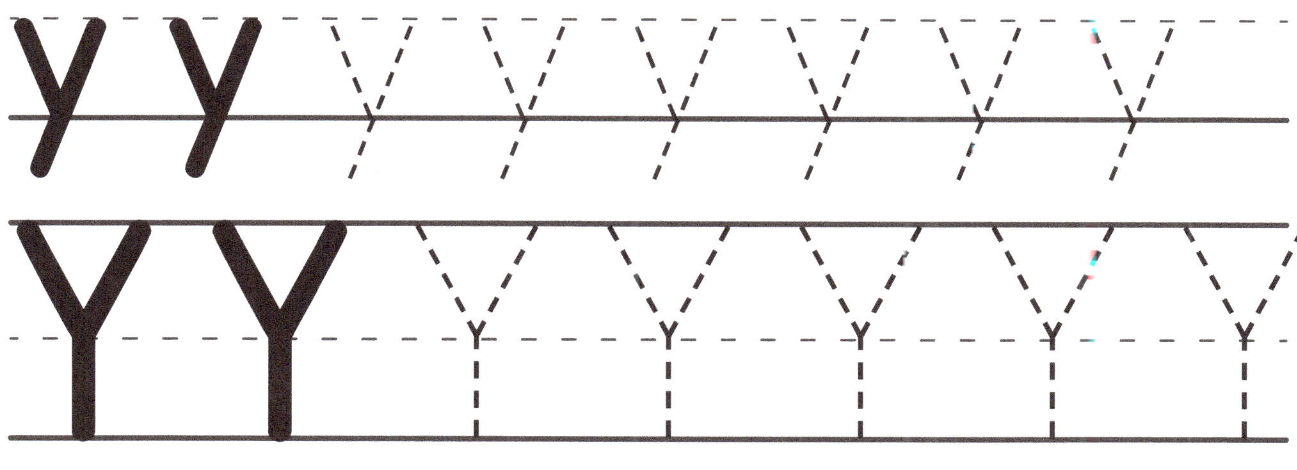

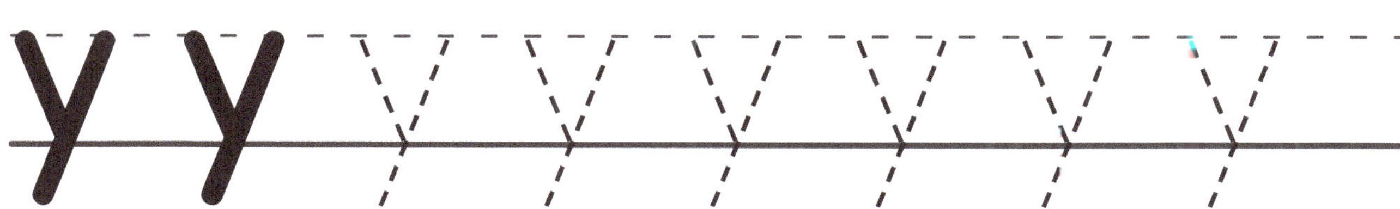

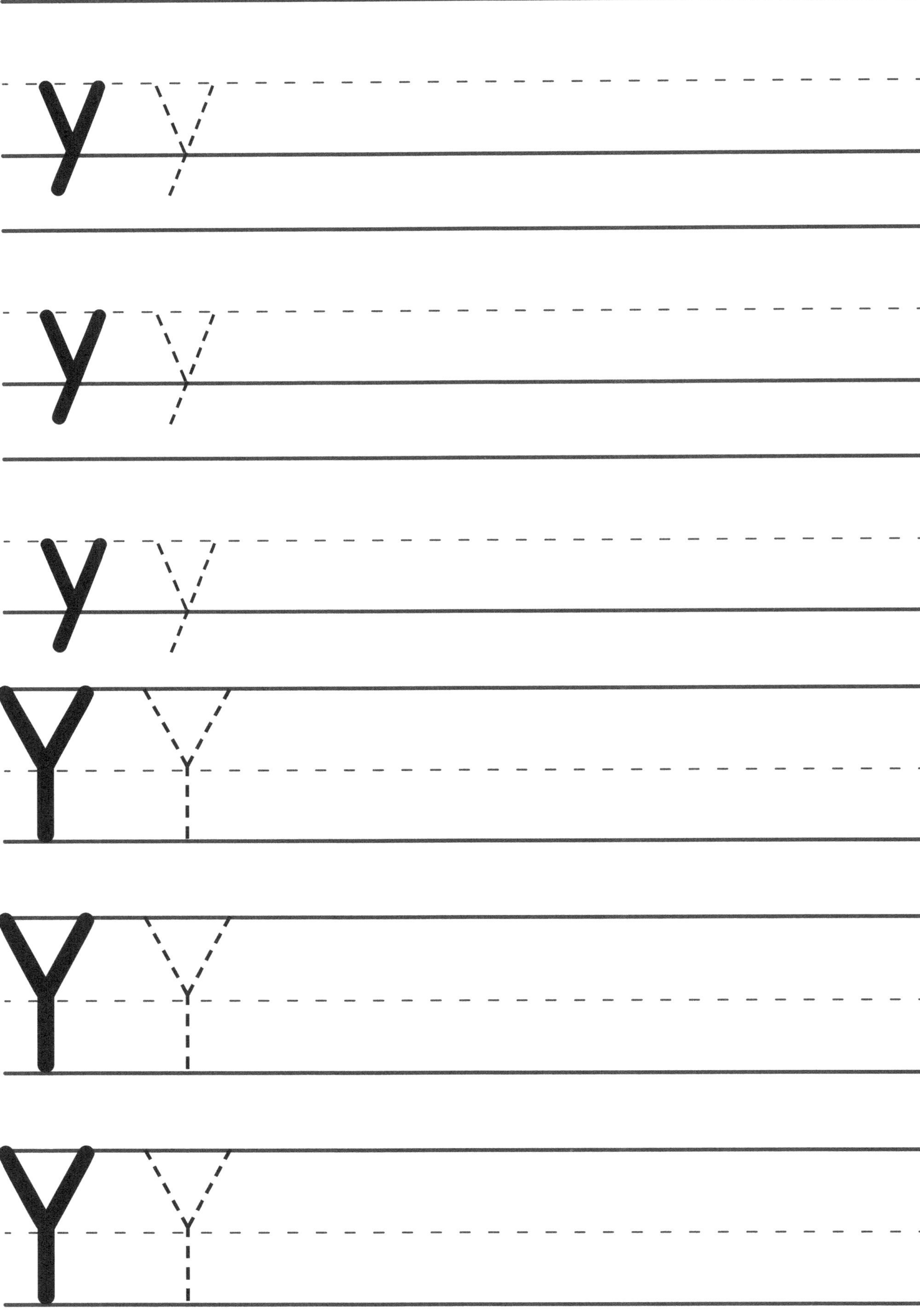

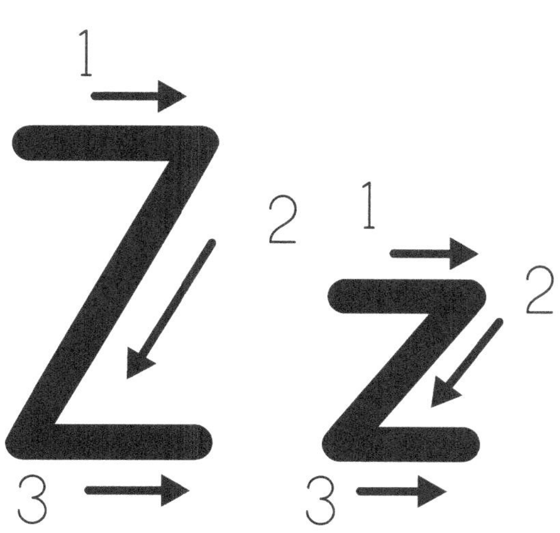

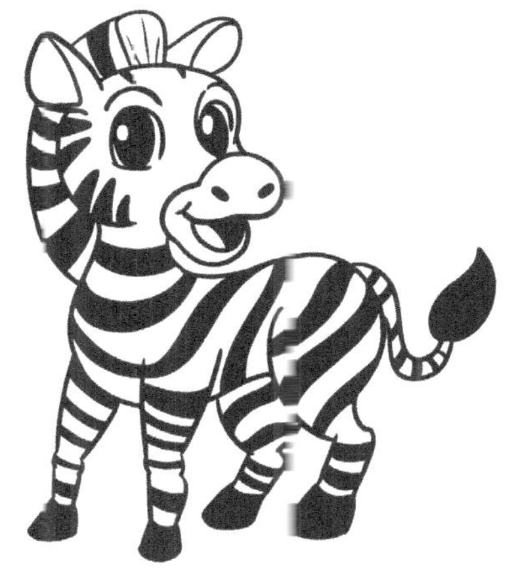

Zebra

Zebra

z z

Z Z

z z

Z

Z

Z

Z

Z

Z

Sight Words

Learn to read

Aa is for...

Trace the word and say it out loud:

a a a a a a

Write the word:

Trace the word and say it out loud:

as as as as

Write the word:

Trace the word and say it out loud:

and and and

Write the word:

Bb is for...

Trace the word and say it out loud:

be   be be be

Write the word:

Trace the word and say it out loud:

but   but but

Write the word:

Trace the word and say it out loud:

been   been

Write the word:

Cc is for...

Trace the word and say it out loud:

can can can

Write the word:

Trace the word and say it out loud:

come come

Write the word:

Trace the word and say it out loud:

could could

Write the word:

Dd is for...

Trace the word and say it out loud:

do   do   do   do

Write the word:

Trace the word and say it out loud:

does   does

Write the word:

Trace the word and say it out loud:

down   down

Write the word:

Ee is for...

Trace the word and say it out loud:

eat   eat   eat

Write the word:

Trace the word and say it out loud:

ear   ear   ear

Write the word:

Trace the word and say it out loud:

each   each

Write the word:

Ff is for...

Trace the word and say it out loud:

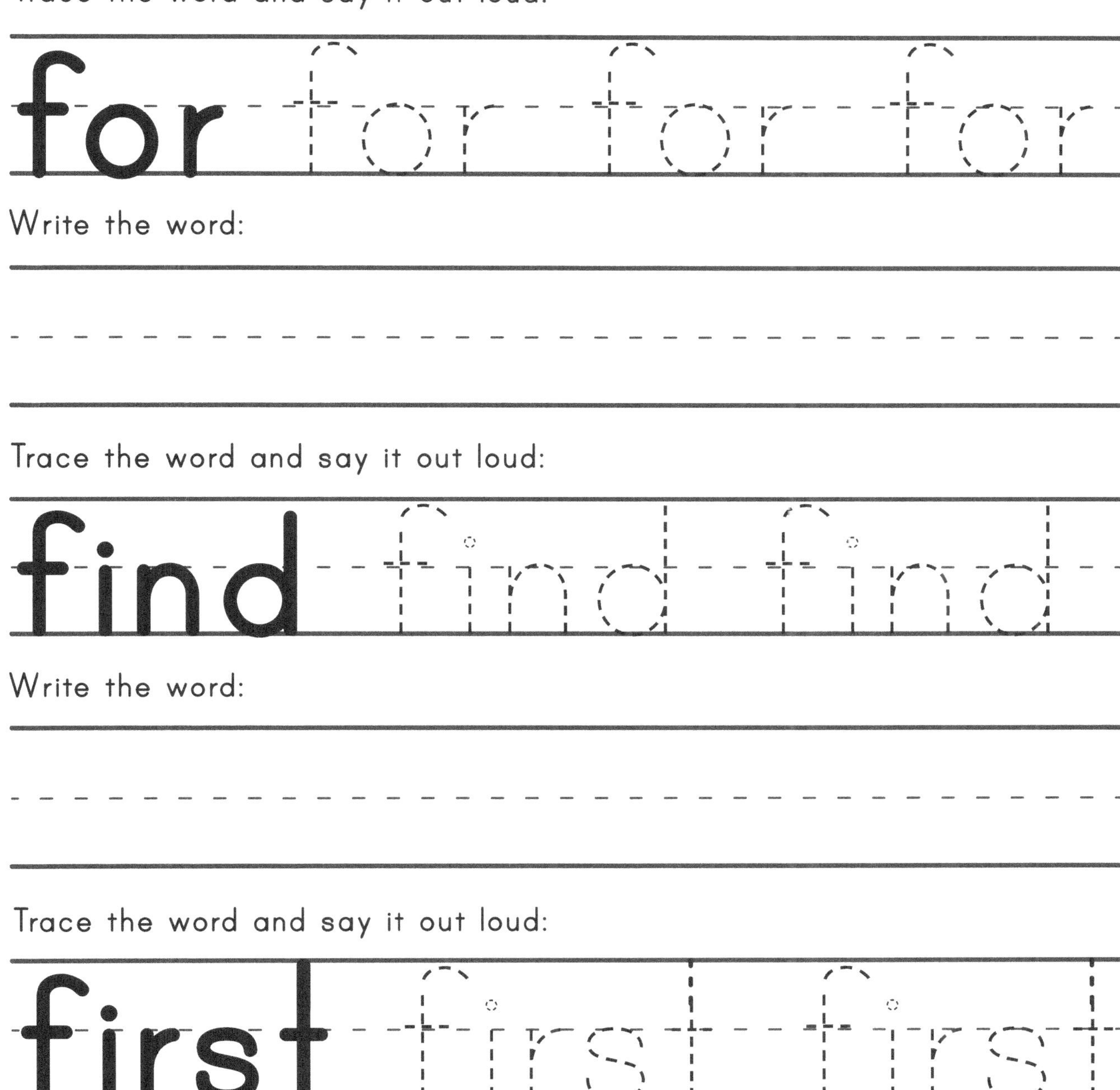

Write the word:

Trace the word and say it out loud:

Write the word:

Trace the word and say it out loud:

Write the word:

Gg is for...

Trace the word and say it out loud:

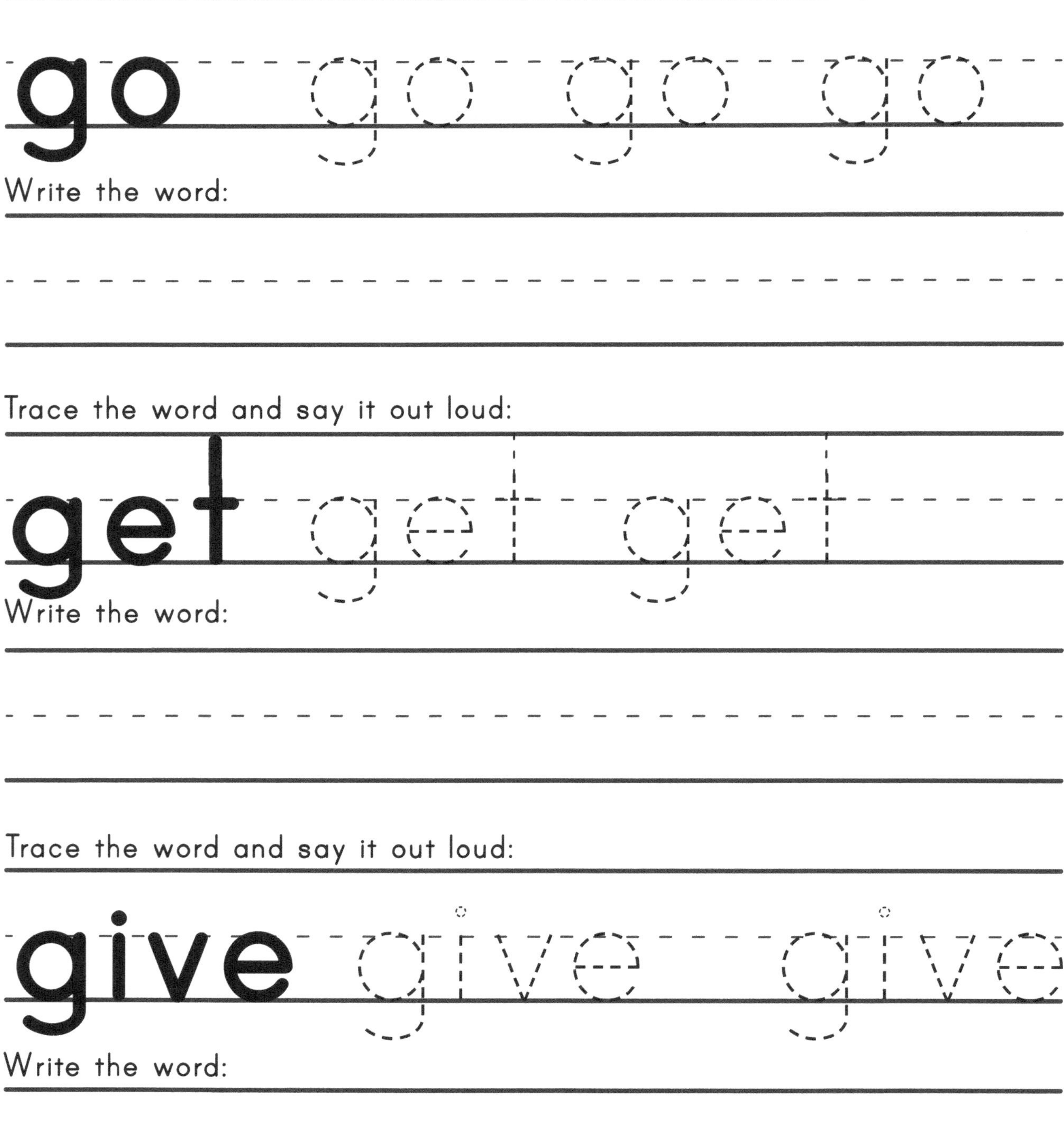

go

Write the word:

Trace the word and say it out loud:

get

Write the word:

Trace the word and say it out loud:

give

Write the word:

Hh is for...

Trace the word and say it out loud:

he

Write the word:

Trace the word and say it out loud:

has

Write the word:

Trace the word and say it out loud:

her

Write the word:

Ii is for...

Trace the word and say it out loud:

in   in in in in in

Write the word:

Trace the word and say it out loud:

is   is is is is is

Write the word:

Trace the word and say it out loud:

if   if if if if if if

Write the word:

Jj is for...

Trace the word and say it out loud:

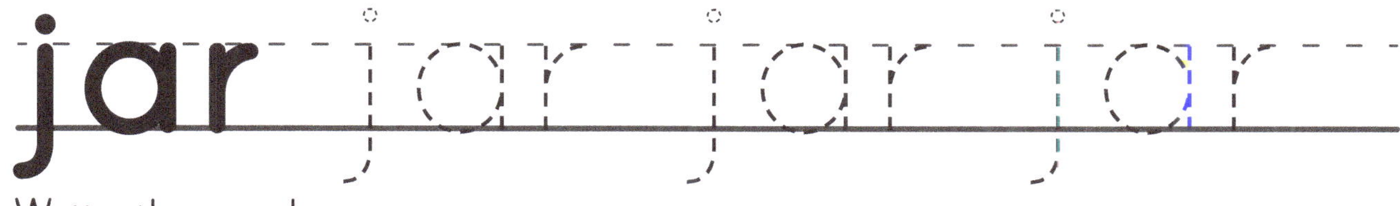

Write the word:

Trace the word and say it out loud:

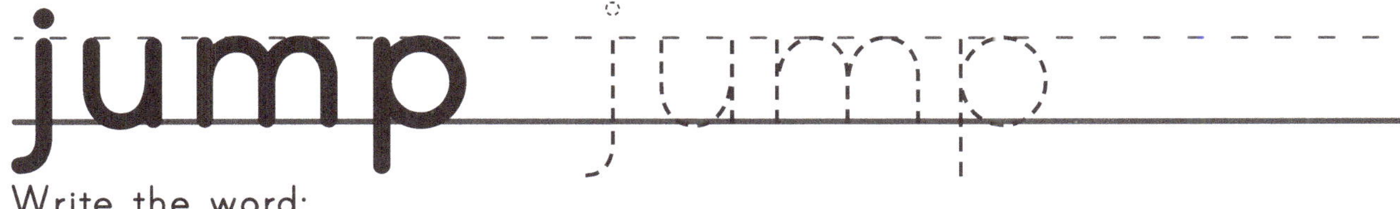

Write the word:

Trace the word and say it out loud:

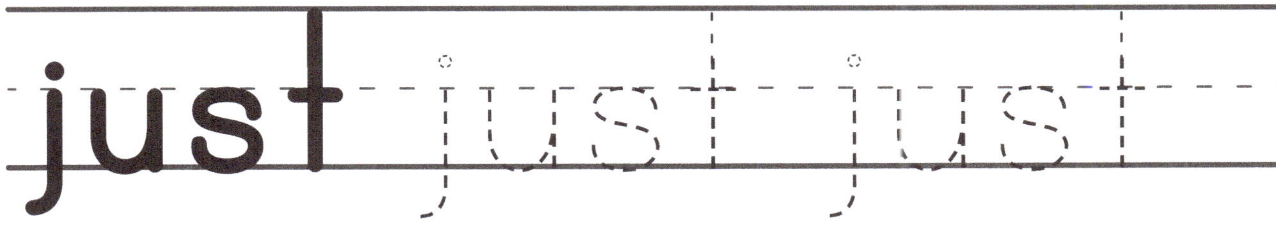

Write the word:

Kk is for...

Trace the word and say it out loud:

key   key   key

Write the word:

Trace the word and say it out loud:

kick   kick   kick

Write the word:

Trace the word and say it out loud:

know   know

Write the word:

Ll is for...

Trace the word and say it out loud:

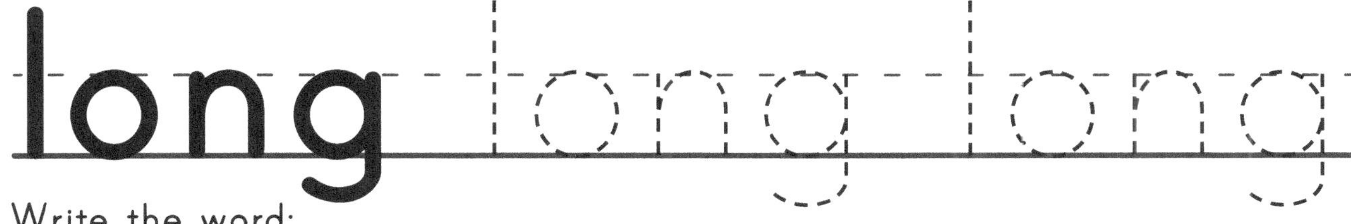

Write the word:

Trace the word and say it out loud:

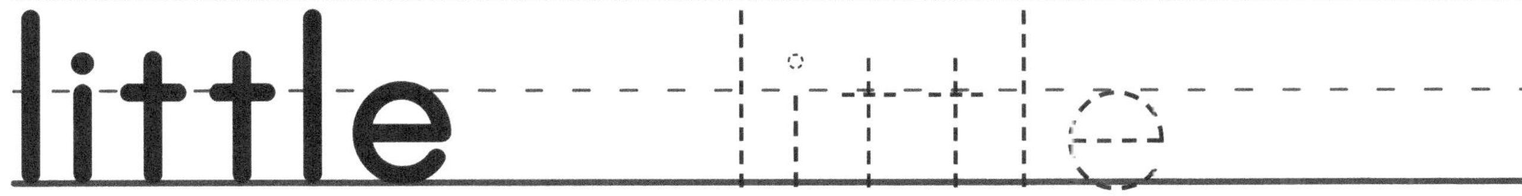

Write the word:

Trace the word and say it out loud:

little   little

Write the word:

Mm is for...

Trace the word and say it out loud:

more   more

Write the word:

____

Trace the word and say it out loud:

make   make

Write the word:

____

Trace the word and say it out loud:

must   must

Write the word:

____

Nn is for...

Trace the word and say it out loud:

no   no no no

Write the word:

Trace the word and say it out loud:

not   not   not

Write the word:

Trace the word and say it out loud:

new   new

Write the word:

Oo is for...

Trace the word and say it out loud:

of   of of of of

Write the word:

Trace the word and say it out loud:

on   on on on

Write the word:

Trace the word and say it out loud:

out   out out

Write the word:

Pp is for...

Trace the word and say it out loud:

put

Write the word:

Trace the word and say it out loud:

play

Write the word:

Trace the word and say it out loud:

place

Write the word:

Qq is for...

Trace the word and say it out loud:

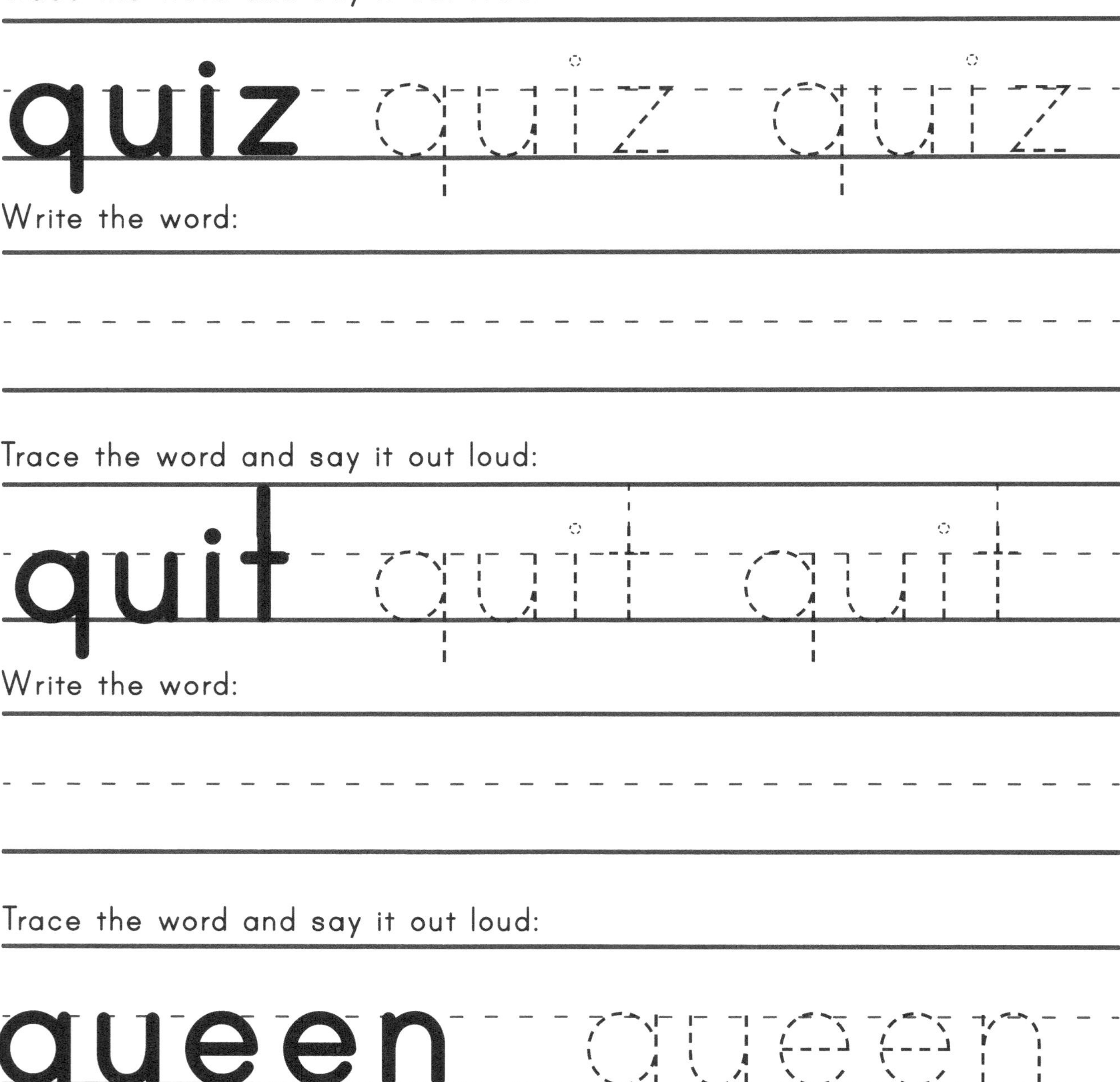

Write the word:

Trace the word and say it out loud:

Write the word:

Trace the word and say it out loud:

Write the word:

Rr is for...

Trace the word and say it out loud:

red   red   red

Write the word:

Trace the word and say it out loud:

run   run   run

Write the word:

Trace the word and say it out loud:

read   read

Write the word:

Ss is for...

Trace the word and say it out loud:

so so so so

Write the word:

Trace the word and say it out loud:

said said said

Write the word:

Trace the word and say it out loud:

see see see

Write the word:

Tt is for...

Trace the word and say it out loud:

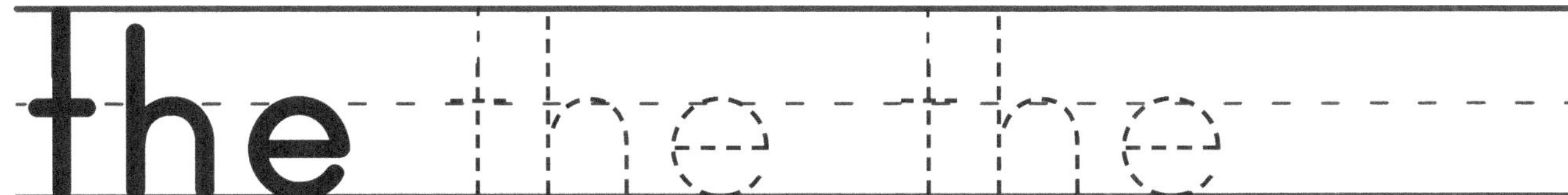

Write the word:

Trace the word and say it out loud:

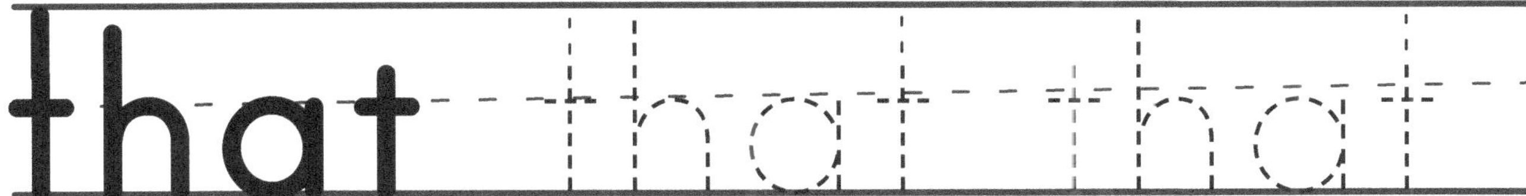

Write the word:

Trace the word and say it out loud:

that that that

Write the word:

Uu is for...

Trace the word and say it out loud:

up   up   up

Write the word:

Trace the word and say it out loud:

use   use

Write the word:

Trace the word and say it out loud:

under   under

Write the word:

Vv is for...

Trace the word and say it out loud:

van van van

Write the word:

Trace the word and say it out loud:

vase vase vase

Write the word:

Trace the word and say it out loud:

video video

Write the word:

Ww is for...

Trace the word and say it out loud:

we we we we

Write the word:

Trace the word and say it out loud:

was was was

Write the word:

Trace the word and say it out loud:

what what

Write the word:

Xx is for...

Trace the word and say it out loud:

x-ray   x-ray

Write the word:

Trace the word and say it out loud:

box   box   box

Write the word:

Trace the word and say it out loud:

fox   fox   fox

Write the word:

Yy is for...

Trace the word and say it out loud:

you *you you*

Write the word:

Trace the word and say it out loud:

yes *yes yes*

Write the word:

Trace the word and say it out loud:

your *your your*

Write the word:

Zz is for...

Trace the word and say it out loud:

zoo zoo zoo

Write the word:

Trace the word and say it out loud:

zero zero zero

Write the word:

Trace the word and say it out loud:

zebra zebra

Write the word:

Practice!

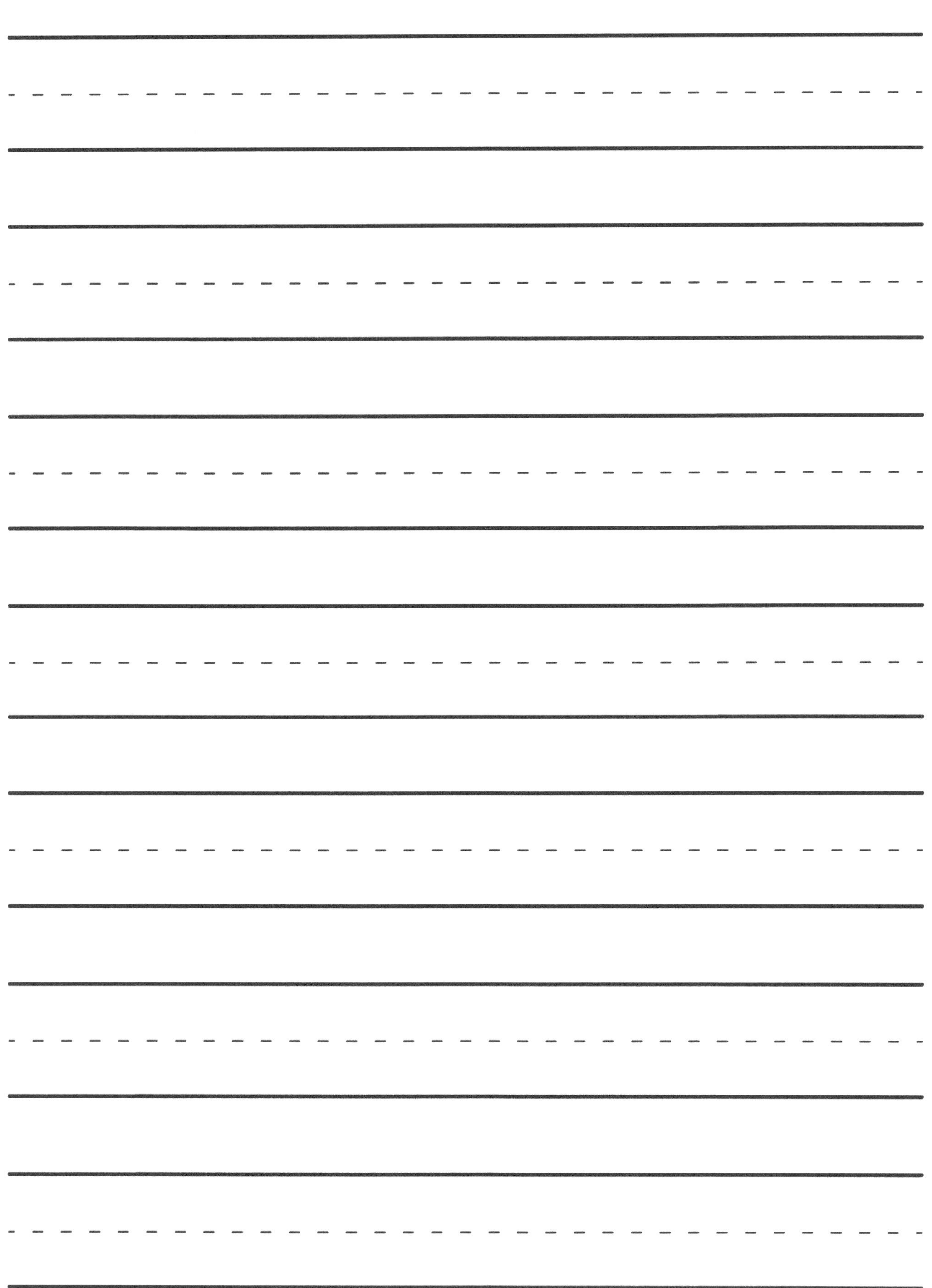

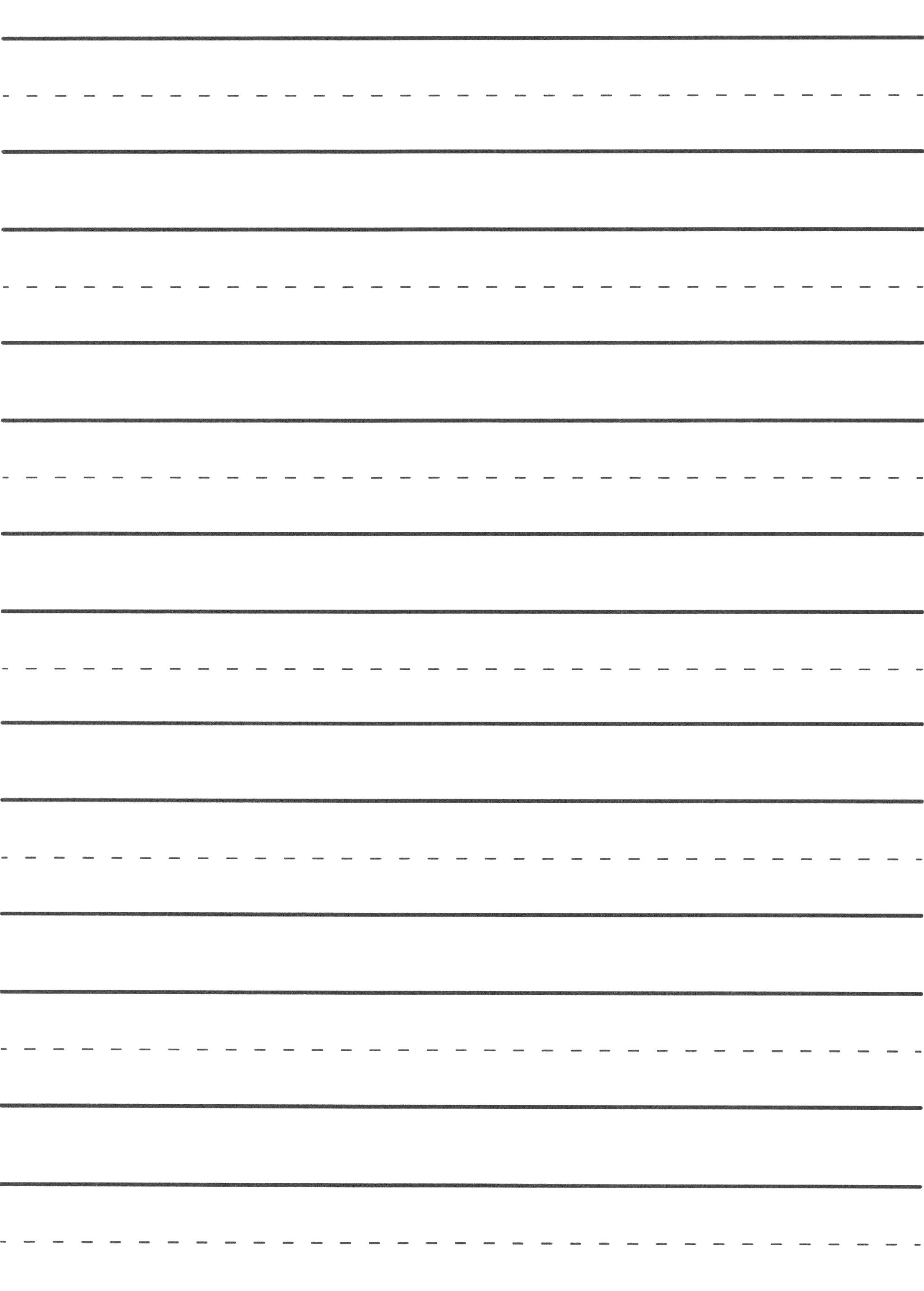